2020

HISTORIC PHOTOS OF
BROADWAY

NEW YORK THEATER, 1850–1970

TEXT AND CAPTIONS BY LEONARD JACOBS
IMAGES FROM THE BILLY ROSE THEATRE DIVISION,
THE NEW YORK PUBLIC LIBRARY FOR THE PERFORMING ARTS

TURNER
PUBLISHING COMPANY

George Kelly (1887-1974) wrote plays that made audiences laugh and think. *The Torch Bearers* (1922) parodied the Little Theatre movement that arose after World War I. *The Show Off* (1924), his next play, starred Louis John Bartels (1895-1932) as Aubrey Piper, a man whose capacity for egocentrism far exceeds his station in life. By far Kelly's most popular play (with more than 500 performances in its original Broadway run, and New York revivals in 1937, 1950, 1967, and 1992), the Pulitzer committee passed over *The Show Off*, awarding Hatcher Hughes' *Hell Bent for Heaven* instead. The Rialto's hue and cry was long and loud until the next year, when Kelly won for *Craig's Wife* (1925). This shot was taken on February 5, 1925, at the Playhouse Theatre—the first anniversary of *The Show Off* 's original run. Kelly was credited by his niece, Grace Kelly, for encouraging her to go into acting.

HISTORIC PHOTOS OF BROADWAY

NEW YORK THEATER, 1850–1970

Turner Publishing Company
200 4th Avenue North • Suite 950
Nashville, Tennessee 37219
(615) 255-2665

www.turnerpublishing.com

Historic Photos of Broadway
New York Theater, 1850–1970

Library of Congress Control Number: 2007929566

ISBN-13: 978-1-59652-362-3

Printed in the United States of America

08 09 10 11 12 13 14 15—0 9 8 7 6 5 4 3 2 1

CONTENTS

ACKNOWLEDGMENTS

Historic Photos of Broadway is the result of the cooperation and efforts of many individuals, organizations, and corporations. It is with great thanks that we acknowledge the valuable contribution of the following for their generous support:

This volume would have been impossible without the support of colleagues, friends, and family. Deepest thanks to my publisher, Todd Bottorff, whose tireless efforts on behalf of this volume afforded me this opportunity. My heartfelt gratitude to Turner Publishing's staff: Steven Cox, my editor, who applied a terrific pair of eagle eyes to the style, voice, tone, and spirit of this book; Heather Watson, project assistant, who shepherded the promotional copy; David Latta, project designer, whose peerless design sense brought 240 images to life; and Gene Bedell, production manager, whose unflappable grace and professionalism during the production process was a gift to us all.

The staff of the Billy Rose Theatre Division, The New York Public Library for the Performing Arts, has been a consistent source of insight and information. Heading the list is photo librarian Jeremy Megraw, whose ceaseless efforts and contributions cannot be overstated. Thanks, too, to the library's excellent staff: Roderick L. Bladel, Christopher J. Frith, Christine A. Karatnytsky, Annette C. Marotta, Louise Martzinek, Stephen C. Massa, Karen Nickeson, and Olive T. Wong. Notes of appreciation to: Brian Scott Lipton, my longtime friend and mentor, for overall advice; Erik Haagensen, my colleague and friend at *Back Stage,* for invaluable information on musical theater and for helping me to identify many individuals in photographs; Sue Viera of U.P.S. for finding a needle in a haystack; and the staff of the Village Copier. Special thanks to Don Wilmeth, Brown University Professor Emeritus, whose mentorship and friendship remain invaluable to me.

Very special thanks to Stephen Van Gorden, whose enthusiasm, research, organization, patience, prescience, gut instincts, untapped knowledge, and friendship proved instrumental to this book. The love of my parents, Edward and JoAnn Jacobs, my grandmother, Helene Blank, and especially my partner, Ken Koranyi, always kept me grounded, gratified, and inspired.

This book is dedicated to the memory of my grandfather, Herbert M. Faitt, whose greatest gift to me was a lifelong love of history.

About The Billy Rose Theatre Division

The Billy Rose Theatre Division, The New York Public Library for the Performing Arts, is the world's largest archive devoted to the documentation of theater. Its holdings number around 9 million items and about one-third of them are photographs. A good writer with a sharp eye and a gift for adjectives could describe in detail what he saw last night onstage at the Bijou. But accurate as that description might be, every reader would visualize it differently. Not so with a photograph. Although, in the last several years, technology has provided easy means for photographic prevarication, this was not always the case; in early photographs, the photographer's greatest sin might have been air-brushing a double chin or two. Fortunately, most of the three million or so photographs in the Billy Rose Theatre Division are, decidedly, "early" and, it is fairly certain, visually trustworthy. The 240 images in this book have been drawn preponderantly from three separate collections of photographs held by the Billy Rose Theatre Division: the White Studio Collection, the Vandamm Collection, and the Friedman-Abeles Collection.

The White Studio photographed almost 90 percent of all live performance in New York between 1904 and 1936. More than 100,000 images provide, in many cases, the only existing visual documentation of plays, vaudeville acts, concerts, and dance during that unusually rich period of American performing arts. These photographs are highly prized by theater historians around the world. By the time the White Studio shut its doors in 1936, the Vandamm Studio had been nipping at its heels for some years and was now to the fore in the field of theater photography. From the late 1920s through the early 1960s, Florence and Tommy Vandamm photographed virtually every important show that opened in New York and every performer who appeared onstage—nearly 50,000 images of more than 8,000 shows. The Billy Rose Theatre Division acquired this matchless collection from Florence Vandamm shortly before she retired in 1961. In 1992, the Theatre Division acquired the largest of its collections of photographs. The Friedman-Abeles Studio dominated theatrical photography from the mid-1950s through the mid-1970s, and, by the time it closed shop, the studio had accumulated nearly 600,000 images. During its twenty-year run, the Friedman-Abeles Studio photographed not only thousands of legitimate stage productions—in New York and around the country—but also hundreds of special events such as opening night parties and the Tony Awards. This collection is further enriched by thousands of rehearsal shots and back-stage candids.

Each of these three collections of photographs is in great demand by researchers because, together, they constitute a unique and reliable visual record of theater in New York for three-quarters of the twentieth century. The Billy Rose Theatre Division is proud to be the custodian of this unrivaled photographic archive and grateful to Leonard Jacobs and Turner Publishing for helping us share the glorious history of New York theater.

Bob Taylor
Lewis and Dorothy Cullman Curator, Billy Rose Theatre Division
The New York Public Library for the Performing Arts

PREFACE

I write this in the wintertime, when the New York City light is substantively different from its appearance at other times of the year. Especially below 14th Street, in the older, more history-rich sections of Manhattan, in addition to being genuinely beautiful, the city's architecture exerts impulses toward introspection and retrospection. I ponder the way it all must have looked 100 or 150 years ago, or even earlier. I shut my eyes and try listening for long-vanished sounds—for the metronomic clop-clop clop-clop of horses on cobblestone.

And as the theater is my first love, I listen especially for the sounds of the stage: the courtly applause of immaculately dressed gentlemen; the high-pitched giggle of matinee ladies in the full tilt of rapture with a play. I listen for the dainty feet of ruffle-and-lace dancers scurrying from tiny, chilly dressing rooms to the metal stairs they clack down in unison as they assume their positions behind the curtain. I listen intently for the Shakespeare of Booth and of Barrymore, of dramatic speech once considered brilliant and perhaps construable as such today. I yearn to hear the startled reactions of the audience to everything that was thrillingly new: hearts beating faster as chorines, perfect legs for miles, bedazzled in their perfect choreographic harmony; gasps at the realistic, naturalistic social dramas that dragged controversial social topics out of cigar-filled drawing rooms, repackaging them into the DNA of supreme drama; the pleasant and satisfied humming of melodies direct from the musical theater, ever-mystical in its ability to whisk one away from daily cares.

Opening my eyes, I remain below 14th Street. It's still winter, and few traces of the New York theater of a century or more ago survive today. Taking a quick subway ride uptown, to the hurlyburly of Times Square, change is everywhere in evidence—so many brainless, bland, blah-looking skyscraper condos replacing beloved watering holes, rehearsal spaces, eateries, and apartments and even so many of the theaters, demolished long ago, that helped to make Broadway the epicenter of the theatrical world. We can close our eyes all we want, listen all we want, but finally we must awaken to our present world. We must know that all we really have is our imagination, our ability to picture things as they were in the New York light, to not forget what once stood where.

This is why photography for me is a window into a theater world of people, places, and plays I can never completely know. Through photography one can get pretty close.

And that's why I have written this book. As curator Bob Taylor details, the Billy Rose Theatre Division, The New York Public Library for the Performing Arts, is one of the grandest, most diverse repositories of theatrical memorabilia in the world; fully a third of its nine million items are photographs. So it seemed to me if we no longer can locate traces of yesteryear's theater outside, photographs are the best way to keep memories and histories of the theater close by. But what story to tell? It seemed to me that the first story to tell, if in only a somewhat broad way, would be the story of Broadway. It's as much a metaphor, an idea, a symbol, a brand, a destination, as it is a long, jagged thoroughfare extending nearly 150 miles from Bowling Green in lower Manhattan, to Albany, capital of New York State.

Historic Photos of Broadway begins before the Civil War—the first image shows legendary actor Edwin Booth as a young man reverently standing beside his father, equally acclaimed actor Junius Brutus Booth. Although the photograph's exact date cannot be pinpointed, suffice it to say that the Booths are one possible way to evoke the world of the New York stage (and the American stage) before the Civil War. Owing to President Lincoln's assassination by Edwin's brother, John Wilkes, the photograph also helps to characterize and contextualize the New York stage after the Civil War. The following 239 photographs represent my attempt to construct a photographic history of Broadway to 1970, showcasing the most spectacular elements of the library's holdings. I will be the first to agree that this book is as much about inclusion as about exclusion, that it's neither complete nor thorough. However, I hope you will agree that finding 240 photographs out of 3 million in order to encapsulate 120 years of history is a tall order. And that this survey is a good start.

Meanwhile, the more I research, the more I become convinced that it's virtually impossible to present the theater of yesteryear in a real, visceral way for today's eyes, ears, and tastes. Although we can gain access to many of the superficial aspects of the theatergoing experience, such as dress and decorum, through history books and first-person accounts, many elements of the theater of yore will never seem anything less than quaint and antiquated. But for me, many of these photographs bring us just a little bit closer to what we cannot intimately know. If we really could use these images to transport ourselves back 100 years or more, it's unlikely we'd be as enraptured with the machinery of melodrama or of well-made plays as our forebears. We might realize that like our forebears, we attend theater principally to be entertained. So I also hope you find this volume full of pure pleasure, too.

These images ask us not to judge and not to linger. They simply ask us to pay a visit, tip our hats in respect, and take the full measure of our present moment in the theater by sneaking a quick peek through that metaphorical window to the past. These images permit us to shut our eyes yet one more time and try to picture that past. They also let us celebrate our present and they ultimately demand that we press on, to welcome the future with fully open arms.

On a final note, a diligent effort has been made to include the birth and death dates of all theatrical persons crossing this book's stage. Plays likewise are dated, either with year of creation or year of Broadway opening. Dates are given with first references only.

British-born Junius Brutus Booth (1796-1852) and his son Edwin (1833-93) symbolized great nineteenth-century American acting. The younger Booth would eventually outshine his father to become the century's finest actor. His brother, John Wilkes (1838-65), also an actor, assassinated President Lincoln in 1865.

PRE- AND PROTO-BROADWAY

(1850–1870)

Photographs can impart only a small sense of the mid-nineteenth-century New York theater. Broadway, for example, was still considered a winding thoroughfare rudely interrupting Manhattan's grid, with the world north of 14th Street largely viewed as an urban wilderness.

Roiling politics were rocking the nation: the forces of rapid industrialization, manifest destiny, slavery, and ethnic diversification were all in motion at once, leaving popular culture to quench the thirst for diversion—for the powers of illusion only the theater could provide. In photography, that power could be captured: witness the coy, smiling, bare-shouldered Lydia Thompson in a wicker basket; *The Black Crook*'s bewitching chorus; the comedy of two men called Harrigan and Hart. Arresting images bring the unexpected to modern eyes: San Francisco thespians channeling the Broadway scene by burlesquing a famous photo of Augustin Daly reading a new play to his bored company; a caricature of one of the Kiralfy brothers holding a ballerina pristinely in his palm. Some images are as postmodern-ironic as anything on *The Daily Show.*

Human eyes can also tell tales. Notice Ada Rehan, photographed opposite John Drew, Jr., holding her body neutral yet communicating with the tilt of her head and coquettish eyes the narrative of a scene. Or Henry E. Dixey staring into heavenly bliss as Adonis. Or Lillian Russell leaning against a mirror, her impression doubled.

The very first image printed here—of Junius Brutus Booth and his son, Edwin—finds two great stage actors side-by-side soon after the invention of photography itself. What were they thinking, posing for the newfangled lens? And a decade or so later, when Edwin's brother, John Wilkes, assassinated Abraham Lincoln?

This section also begins a long lament for a New York theater that is lost forever—the commanding frontage of the Academy of Music; the inviting facade of Niblo's Garden; the dramatically lit half of the proscenium arch of the Fifth Avenue Theatre. We can only imagine what plays, stars, and triumphs were seen on the unseen stage, and it is photography that provides the imagination a window.

Some historians call *The Black Crook* (1866) the first American musical comedy. That's not quite accurate, although musical comedy's roots can be traced to it. When backers of a stranded French ballet troupe needed a venue, Niblo's Garden owner-manager William Wheatley (1816-76) bought the troupe and proposed adding music and the more than 100 dancers to a new play by Charles M. Barras (1826-73), an unknown. Wheatley then quelled Barras' protests by paying him $1,500 amid promises of royalties that paid off many times over. Spectacular, titillating, eye-popping—*The Black Crook* ran 475 performances and was revived over and over in New York and around the nation, one of the nineteenth century's biggest hits.

Located on the northeast corner of Broadway and Prince Street, Niblo's Garden had been farmland, then a resort-saloon with a small theater. Eventually its seating capacity topped 3,000 seats and was considered state-of-the-art for its time. It was twice destroyed by fire (in 1846 and 1872) and rebuilt, then demolished in 1895 for an office building. Aside from productions of *The Black Crook* (1866, 1870, 1871), notable Niblo's shows included John Gay's *The Beggar's Opera* (1855, 1859) and Dion Boucicault's *Arrah-Na-Pogue* (1865, 1869).

The chorus of *The Black Crook:*

"Hark, Hark, Hark,
Hark the birds with tuneful voices
Vocal for our Lady Fair
And the lips of op'ning flowers
Breathe their incense on the air
Breathe their incense on the air . . ."

The photograph is by Napoleon Sarony (1821-96), an American photographer known for his exquisite portraits of theater stars.

Bare-shouldered and flirty-eyed, this basketed coquette may look tame to twenty-first-century eyes. But in 1868, when Lydia Thompson (1836-1908) brought her leggy troupe of British blondes to American shores, a blow was struck against the social codes of the day and the American craze for burlesque was born. Historian Cecil Smith (1906-56) noted, "Neither Lydia nor her blondes . . . could act, nor did they pretend to." Their performing style, however, would last well into the next century.

The Academy of Music was one of New York's most beloved and enduring houses. Built in 1854 for opera (a modification of an original structure that had partly burned), it also offered minstrel shows, concerts, plays, musicals, films, and vaudeville. Near the end of its life it housed meetings against Tammany Hall corruption and in favor of organized labor. Opera legend Adelina Patti (1843-1919) sang here; Edwin Booth and Helena Modjeska (1840-1909) acted here; and the first member of the British royal family to visit America, the Prince of Wales, later King Edward VII (1841-1910), was feted here in a dazzling 1860 welcome. When the center of New York theater was on 14th Street near Union Square, the Academy of Music was its crown jewel. It was demolished in 1926 to make way for today's Consolidated Edison building.

Dancer-acrobats Imre (1845-1919), Arnold (184?-1908), and Bolossy Kiralfy (1848-1932, caricatured) arrived in the U.S. in 1868. They debuted with their sisters Haniola (1851-89) and Emilie (1855-1917), in *Hickory Dickory Dock* (1869), a mix of pantomime and spectacle bearing no relation to the Mother Goose tales and was actually a sequel to a 483-performance hit called *Humpty Dumpty* (1868). Such piffle, though, encouraged the men to pursue serious interests, especially when they began producing and innovating stage technology, such as using electricity for lighting. Their 1873 revival of *The Black Crook* and, finally, their production of *Around the World in Eighty Days* (1875) established them as expert purveyors of large-scale pieces that never failed to wow audiences.

Billing their play an "American opéra bouffe" and later an "American extravaganza," Edward E. Rice (1849-1924) and J. Cheever Goodwin (1850-1912) seized upon *The Black Crook*'s innovations and Lydia Thompson–style permissiveness to create *Evangeline; or, The Belle of Acadia* (1874), loosely based on the poem by Henry Wadsworth Longfellow (1807-82). They even persuaded the management of Niblo's Garden that history could repeat itself—and it did: *Evangeline* was almost never out of production for the next 30 years. The dancing heifer in the show—not, alas, the lovely maiden in this image—is the stuff of legend.

The Shaughraun (1874) was one of the finest plays by Dion Boucicault (1820-90). It's a melodrama about Robert Folliott, a fugitive Irish nationalist; his fiancée, Arte O'Neil; and Kinchela, the squire vying for her hand using any means available, including a police informer or Shaughraun (a wanderer, played by Boucicault). Pictured are H. J. Montague (1843-78) and Ada Dyas (1843-1908) of the original production. Dyas played Robert's sister and Montague the English soldier she falls in love with—whose job is to locate fugitives. As for what happens, well, one would just have to see the play.

I am the boy
Charles E Wallack
Rockwood
1409 Broadway,
S.W. cor. 39th St, N.Y.

The boy at center stands between generations of a major theatrical family. On the left, Lester Wallack (1820-88), an actor adroit at both the plays of William Shakespeare and sophisticated English comedies, and a playwright and theater manager whose stages trained many nineteenth-century and early twentieth century actors. On the right, James William Wallack (1791-1864), Lester's father, often called "the Elder," an actor and theater manager who achieved renown in the U.S. and Great Britain. Synonymous with thespian excellence reaching back to eighteenth-century English forebears, there was also the Elder's brother, Henry John (1790-1870), and Lester's cousin, James William Wallack (1818-73, known as "the Younger"). Five New York theaters bore the Wallack name. Young Charles E. Wallack (?-?), the boy at center, apparently eschewed the family business.

Frank C. Bangs (1833-1908) enjoyed a long career on the stage, largely as a character actor. In 1906, he was struck by a streetcar, which crippled him, it was thought, temporarily. This photograph shows Bangs at his prime, appearing in *Sardanapalus* (1876), a play by Lord Byron (1788-1824).

"H-A-double R-I-G-A-N spells Harrigan" goes a famous lyric tribute to half of Broadway's most beloved musical comedy team. Edward Harrigan (1844-1911) began as a comedian in touring variety shows; he met Hart (1855-91), a reform-school dropout adept at female impersonation, in the mid-1870s. Together they devised sketches speaking directly, hilariously, to New York City's teeming immigrant classes. Stuffed with puns and knockabout humor, Harrigan and Hart's "Mulligan Guard" songs and sketches were a huge attraction—17 full-length musical comedies in under a decade, with music by oft-overlooked composer David Braham (1838-1905). Hart, who left the act in 1885, died of syphilis, never achieving solo success. Harrigan, who wrote their scripts and songs and produced their shows, delighted audiences for another decade.

Curiously, the song "Harrigan" was first heard in a show called *Fifty Miles from Boston* (1908), written by the great George M. Cohan (1878-1942), which ran at the Garrick Theatre. Located at 67 W. 35th Street near present-day Macy's, its original name was Harrigan's Theatre. Built in 1890, Edward Harrigan managed it for just five years; actor Richard Mansfield (1857-1907), producer Charles Frohman (1860-1915), and the Shubert brothers all took turns running the house. Notable plays included *Secret Service* (1896) and *Sherlock Holmes* (1899) by William Gillette (1853-1937); *Captain Jinks of the Horse Marines* (1901) by Clyde Fitch (1865-1909); *Mrs. Warren's Profession* (1905), *Heartbreak House* (1920), and *Saint Joan* (1923) by George Bernard Shaw (1856-1950); *R.U.R.* (1922) by Karel Čapek (1890-1938); *The Adding Machine* (1923) by Elmer Rice (1892-1967); and *The Guardsman* (1925) by Ferenc Molnár (1878-1952), which confirmed Alfred Lunt (1892-1977) and Lynn Fontanne (1887-1983) as Broadway's ace acting team. Before its 1932 demolition, it housed burlesque. A fascinating parking garage stands on the site today.

Augustin Daly (1838-99) was a critic who became a playwright and manager whose stock company revolutionized the stage. Born in North Carolina, educated in Virginia and New York City, Daly became a drama critic at 21. A decade later, he was running his own theater; a decade after that, he was building his own theater. Although his best-known works are *Under the Gaslight* (1867) and *Saratoga* (1870), Daly is typically lauded for his acting company: the hugely popular Ada Rehan (1859-1916); John Drew, Jr. (1853-1927)—uncle of Ethel (1879-1959), John (1882-1942), and Lionel Barrymore (1878-1954); Maude Adams (1872-1953), later the first Peter Pan; and Mrs. Gilbert (1821-1904), whose career lasted nearly 60 years. Adept at melodramas and Shakespeare, Daly's humor was terrific: Below this image are the words "A burlesque of the picture of Augustin Daly reading his play to his company."

A burlesque of the picture of Augustin Daly reading his play to his company. San Francisco, 1892

To Daly's stock company, Ada Rehan and John Drew, Jr., were box-office gold. Born in County Limerick, Ireland, Rehan grew up in Brooklyn. Drew was the son of John Drew, Sr. (1827-62), owner-manager of Philadelphia's Arch Street Theatre with his wife, Louisa Lane Drew (1820-97), where Rehan worked from 1873 to 1875. She spent 20 years with Daly's company until his death in 1899, then acted for another seven years; she was said to have played more than 300 roles and was renowned for Shakespeare. Drew performed in scores of plays in and out of Daly's company, segueing easily between "proper" society and theater folk. The image is from *Dollars and Sense* (1883), Daly's adaptation of a play by German dramatist Adolph L'Arronge (1838-1908).

Mrs. Gilbert, nicknamed Granny, was a colorful woman and fearless character actress. In his memoirs, John Drew, Jr., recalled Daly's troupe, including Gilbert, descending 2,000 feet into a Nevada coal mine to drink champagne. Her final role was in *Granny* (1904), written especially for her by Clyde Fitch. Drew also recalled a supper party honoring British actors Henry Irving (1838-1905) and Ellen Terry (1847-1928) that Mrs. Gilbert attended. Upon entering, Drew kissed Mrs. Gilbert's hand and "Irving, probably thinking that it was rather a formal greeting for people who saw each other every day, said, 'You don't always do that, do you?'

'No, I usually do this.' And I kissed her on the cheek.

This delightful old lady had been 'Grandma' to us all and had been on the stage many years. During the run of *Granny,* she died."

If you're thinking, "Gosh, that man looks like an Adonis," you're right. Henry E. Dixey (1859-1943), widely considered an emblem of nineteenth-century masculine beauty, co-wrote the "burlesque-extravaganza" *Adonis* (1884), with Edward E. Rice of *Evangeline* fame. At 603 performances, *Adonis* was the longest-running show of its time, but its plot is silly: a marble statue comes to life, finds mortals not worth knowing, and returns to being a statue.

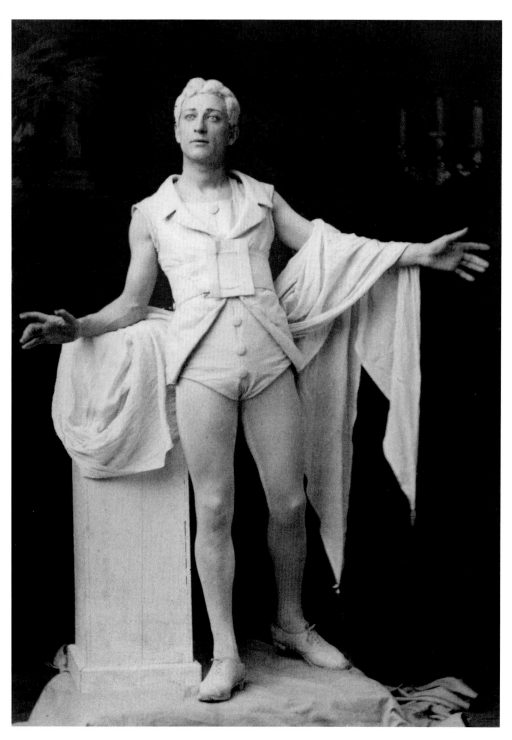

Five-foot-five comedian Digby Bell (1849-1917) was a favorite of the burlesque and operetta era. He's pictured here in the operetta *The Black Hussar* (1884) by Karl Milloecker (1842-99). He starred in the light opera *Jupiter* (1892) and was a featured player in the company of Lillian Russell (1860-1922).

In 1882, James O'Neill (1847-1920) began to play Edmond Dantes in the stage version of *The Count of Monte Cristo* (186?), written by Charles Fechter (1824-79) and based on the Alexandre Dumas (1802-70) novel. He would go on to play the role more than 4,000 times. He was so associated with the role, in fact, that theatergoers nationwide effectively stopped him from tackling other roles. O'Neill was the model for James Tyrone in *Long Day's Journey into Night* (1956), written by his son, Eugene O'Neill (1888-1953).

M'Liss, the Child of the Sierras (1878), based on the short story "Luck of Roaring Camp" by Bret Harte (1837-1902) gave Annie Pixley (1858-93) the signal role of her short career. Raised in California, Pixley and her sisters all pursued stage careers, but only Annie achieved fame. In addition to playing M'Liss for more than a decade, Pixley appeared in *The Deacon's Daughter* (1887) and as Josephine in *HMS Pinafore* (1879) by W. S. Gilbert (1836-1911) and Arthur Sullivan (1842-1900). The Oregon Historical Society, which holds a photo archive of the Pixleys, states that Annie's image as Josephine was also "emblazed on pressed-glass tableware."

The "Divine" Sarah Bernhardt (1844-1923) remains one of the most discussed actresses in history. Bewitching (she was famous for her affairs) and bizarre (she slept in a coffin), her performances in French were intense and audacious: In 1900, at 56, she played Hamlet, among other roles. There were many successful "farewell tours" of the U.S. before her last stateside visit in 1918.

Soon after Edwin Booth's death in 1893, efforts began to cast his likeness in bronze. In 1895, the *New York Times* reported that Riverside Park and Central Park were being considered for the statue, depicting Booth as Hamlet, his most famous role. "It is hoped by the promoters that the statue can be cast in 1896," the *Times* wrote. This photograph, however, records the dedication in Gramercy Park on the 85th anniversary of Booth's birth, November 13, 1918, directly in view of the Players Club, Booth's onetime home. Brander Matthews (1852-1929), the first professor of dramatic literature in any American university (Columbia) and Booth's friend, is speaking at center.

By 1887, when David Belasco (1859-1931) co-authored *The Wife* (with Henry C. DeMille, 1850-93), he was a rising New York figure and had already acted more than 150 roles and written or co-written 100 plays back home in San Francisco. Later plays included *Lord Chumley* (with DeMille, 1888), *Zaza* (1899), *Madame Butterfly* (1900), *DuBarry* (1901), *The Girl of the Golden West* (1905), *The Rose of the Rancho* (1906), and *The Return of Peter Grimm* (1911). He later boasted working on 400 productions or more. In 1907, Belasco built the West 44th Street theater that today bears his name. Belasco's naturalistic insights (for 1912's *The Governor's Lady,* he replicated a Child's restaurant onstage) were ahead of their time. Pictured are *The Wife*'s Georgia Cayvan (1858-1906) and Herbert Kelcey (1855-1917).

Comedy team Joe Weber (1867-1942), left, and Lew Fields (1867-1941) debuted together on the Bowery at age 9. Their act would succeed Harrigan and Hart in the area of knockabout, slapstick comedy with a nod to Lower East Side immigrants—in this case, Germans and Eastern Europeans. In 1896, Weber and Fields' Broadway Music Hall offered musical travesties and burlesques of contemporary plays: "Cyranose de Bric-a-Brac" for *Cyrano de Bergerac;* "Sapolio" for Clyde Fitch's *Sapho;* "The Stickiness of Gelatine" for Fitch's *The Stubbornness of Geraldine.* Fields' children—Dorothy (1905-74), Joseph (1895-1966), and Herbert (1897-1958)—all enjoyed successful theater careers.

Lillian Russell—seen here in *The Queen's Mate* (1888)—was a comic-opera favorite, especially those of W. S. Gilbert and Arthur Sullivan. After she joined Weber and Fields' company, *Whirl-i-gig* (1899), *Fiddle-dee-dee* (1900), *Hoity Toity* (1901), and *Whoop-Dee-Doo* (1903) were all in her debt. The 40-year romance between the quadruple-married Russell and James Buchanan "Diamond Jim" Brady (1856-1917) was legendary. While appearing in Weber and Fields' *Twirly Whirly* (1902), Russell made her only recording: "Come Down Ma Evenin' Star," her signature song.

The Amazons (1894) was the first work by British playwright Arthur Wing Pinero (1855-1934) to run in New York after his *The Second Mrs. Tanqueray* (1893), which had vaulted him into the front rank of dramatists. Pictured is part of *The Amazons'* cast: Katherine Florence (1874-1952), Ferdinand Gottschalk (1858-1944), Georgia Cayvan, Herbert Kelcey, Bessie Tyree (1865-1952), and Fritz Williams (1865-1930).

Pinero's *The Amazons* ran in one of the theaters named Lyceum that has existed in New York City. This one, at 23rd Street and Fourth Avenue (present-day Park Avenue South), was fully electrified, supervised by Thomas Edison (1847-1931) himself. Part of the MetLife building complex stands there today. The theater in this 1870 image, meanwhile, was set to be called the Lyceum by playwright Charles Fechter, who bought it a few years after it was built. Recalled today for writing the version of *The Count of Monte Cristo* that made James O'Neill a star, Fechter defaulted on loans to rehabilitate the house; it was generally called the Fourteenth Street Theatre thereafter. In 1926, after many dark years, it was reopened by Eva Le Gallienne (1899-1991), whose Civic Repertory Theatre added sheen to the New York stage. In 1938, it was demolished.

Not to be confused with Daly's Fifth Avenue Theatre—at 24th Street near Fifth Avenue and Broadway, later the Madison Square—this Fifth Avenue Theatre was on 28th Street and Broadway. Before ending up as a burlesque house, its history was stellar: Gilbert and Sullivan's *The Pirates of Penzance* (1879) world-premiered here; *Princess Ida* (1884), *The Mikado* (1885), and *Ruddigore* (1887) had their first U.S. runs here, as did Minnie Maddern Fiske—always known as Mrs. Fiske (1865-1932)—in *Becky Sharp* (1899) and Richard Mansfield in *The Devil's Disciple* (1897) by George Bernard Shaw. Berenice Abbott (1898-1991) photographed the theater's proscenium arch and chandelier on November 2, 1938, as part of the Federal Art Project. The theater was demolished a year later.

THE FIN DE SIÈCLE APPROACHES

(1870–1910)

This group of images suggests some of the enormous changes taking place in the New York theater, onstage and off, as the nineteenth century began to look increasingly toward the oncoming twentieth. One shot, a personal favorite, was recorded from the stage of the Broadway Theatre—not the one currently standing at the northern tip of the theater district, but the one that stood briefly at the tip of the Flatiron district, 25 blocks south. It shows well-dressed ticket holders, in their 1895 finery, looking up at the camera from their seats.

Similarly fascinating are many of the individual artists depicted in this section. Minnie Maddern Fiske, for example, whose approach to acting would come to revolutionize the craft, and her husband, Harrison Grey Fiske, publisher of the *New York Dramatic Mirror,* a broadsheet that enthusiastically and unstintingly covered all the art and scandals of the day. Plays by the likes of Shaw, Wilde, and Barrie were crossing the Atlantic for the first time now, and the actors who headlined in them—Richard Mansfield, Maude Adams—are all represented here. There are, as well, some intriguing surprises.

And then there are curiosities. Take a look at the photo of John Drew, Jr., and Maude Adams in *Christopher, Jr.:* Why on earth is he holding a hammer? How unbearably hot was that costume from *Babes in Toyland?* And what is author-director David Belasco instructing actress Frances Starr to do?

One excellent feature of the Billy Rose collection is its images of theater buildings and interiors: the dazzling facade of the fine Liberty Theatre, illuminated in a patriotic, World War I salute; the pristine elegance of the Maxine Elliott's Theatre; the enormous crowd gathered outside the Empire Theatre; the stunning baroque interior of the Century Theatre; the Moorish exterior of the Casino; and the beaux arts delirium of the Lyceum, still standing proud on West 45th Street.

Mrs. Fiske debuted at age three—in Shakespeare—and never looked back. Her realistic acting—here she's Tess in an adaptation of *Tess of the D'Urbervilles* (1902), the novel by Thomas Hardy (1840-1928)—earned fervent admirers. And though her acting in the plays of Henrik Ibsen (1828-1906) was eye-opening, startling, mesmerizing, she was also regularly criticized for lazy diction. *Becky Sharp* (1899), *The New York Idea* (1906), *Salvation Nell* (1908), and *Mrs. Bumpstead-Leigh* (1911) were all Broadway triumphs for her. Redheaded and fiery, Fiske long fought the Syndicate—the monopoly of managers who controlled most of the nation's theaters. Barred from the Syndicate's houses, Fiske played hundreds of small towns instead. Her husband, Harrison Grey Fiske (1861-1942), owned and edited the *New York Dramatic Mirror,* the leading theatrical broadsheet of the era.

Harrison Grey Fiske was already a newspaper man before reaching his majority. At 18, he began writing for the *New York Dramatic Mirror;* by 1888, he edited and owned the broadsheet outright. In 1890, he married Minnie Maddern. Besides stage chronicling, he was a writer, director, producer, and manager, taking over the Manhattan Theatre for several years to promote his wife and her company.

From a time when photography was still labor-intensive, it's unusual to see a shot of an audience from the stage. The reverse of this image says it was taken in 1895 at a benefit performance for a stock company.

At 15, Viola Allen (1869-1948) replaced an established star, Annie Russell (1864-1936), in a road company of *Esmeralda* (1881)—by "Little Lord Fauntleroy" scribe Frances Hodgson Burnett (1849-1924) and actor-playwright William Gillette—and stage history was made. Schooled in the classics by her father (a minor character actor), Allen was renowned for Shakespeare: her Desdemona, Cordelia, Juliet, and Rosalind packed theaters for years. She was the first Gwendolyn in the New York premiere of *The Importance of Being Earnest* (1895) by Oscar Wilde (1854-1900) and acted in several plays by Clyde Fitch. She is pictured here playing Gertrude in *Shenandoah* (1889) by Bronson Howard (1842-1908), opposite actor Henry Miller (1858-1926).

The Star famously housed the Wallacks' stock company for two generations; it was opened in 1861 by James W. Wallack, who named it for himself. Later, his son Lester managed it. Sarah Bernhardt also made her first U.S. appearance here. In 1902, it was demolished; a video of the demolition exists on the Internet site YouTube.

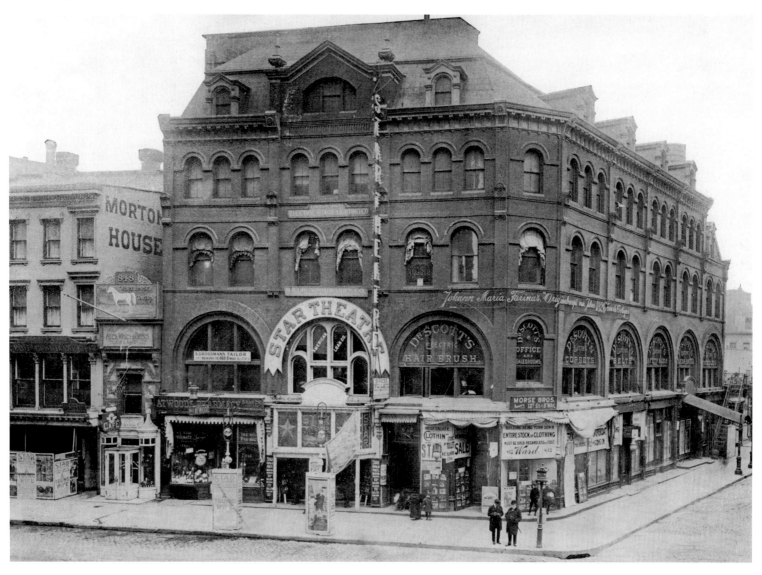

Popular success, critical revulsion—
Clyde Fitch, who wrote more than
60 plays, faced both. Actor-manager
Richard Mansfield hired him to
write *Beau Brummell* (1890), and
that presaged his reputation as a
playwright to the stars: Maude
Adams, John Drew, Jr., Maxine
Elliott (1868-1940), Nat Goodwin
(1857-1919), Julia Marlowe
(1866-1950) all acted in his plays,
as did John Barrymore and Ethel
Barrymore. Largely directing and
designing his own work, Fitch,
whose sartorial flamboyance was
impossible not to notice, once had
four shows running on Broadway
simultaneously. Critics, however,
acidly attacked him, openly
contemptuous of Fitch's thinly
veiled homosexuality, his plays'
melodramatic tics, and his gift for
writing roles for women.

Clyde Fitch's *Beau Brummell* (1890) opened at the Madison Square Theatre, located on West 24th Street near Broadway. On the site had been Augustin Daly's Fifth Avenue Theatre, which burned down in 1873. Opened in 1879 by playwright Steele MacKaye (1842-94), the Madison Square was a technological marvel, with gas lights, folding chairs, rudimentary air-conditioning—using ice blocks, a blower, and subterranean vents to circulate cool air—as well as an elevated orchestra pit and a famous "double stage."

Richard Mansfield was renowned for Shakespeare and the emerging classics of the fin de siècle. Born in Berlin, he was educated in England, where by 1879 he toured in Gilbert and Sullivan's *HMS Pinafore.* In the U.S., Mansfield played operetta, but turned to plays, scoring big in the title roles of Dr. Jekyll and Mr. Hyde and managing his own company. He also launched Clyde Fitch's career by commissioning *Beau Brummell* (1890) and later played two great Shaw characters: Captain Bluntschli in *Arms and the Man* (1894, pictured) and Dick Dudgeon in *The Devil's Disciple* (1897). Personally, Mansfield was ferociously imperious. In his book *Broadway,* critic Brooks Atkinson (1894-1984) wrote, "His ego was so massive and his temper so quick and savage that some people suspected that he was insane."

Farce holds a special place in New York theater. And few outranked in popularity *Charley's Aunt* (1892) by Brandon Thomas (1850-1914). Its plot, involving dual romances and mistaken identities, has served as the template for countless imitations. Pictured are actors Henry Woodruff (1869-1916) as Charles Wykeham, Percy Lyndal (?-?), and Etienne Girardot (1856-1939) as Lord Fancourt Babberley.

London was agog over Oscar Wilde's *Lady Windermere's Fan* (1892), but when it premiered in Boston and New York the following year, stateside critics were ambivalent: the *New York Times* called it "clever and interesting, if neither profound nor particularly wise." The actors were praised, but when Maurice Barrymore (1847-1905), as Lord Darlington, "makes love to another gentleman's wife in the manner of a foreman of a fire-engine company calling for another line of hose, we do not exactly like him." Barrymore appears to be in the center of the photo.

For 50 years, the august William Winter (1836-1917) chronicled the stage, the last 40 with the *New York Tribune.* But Winter was a discontent, as critic Brooks Atkinson noted in his book, *Broadway:* "He had a scowling face with drooping lines, a long scraggly white moustache, and long white hair that was carelessly combed. He looked like a surprised but doleful dolphin. . . . His principal reviews were about 3,400 words in length, set in small type in double-column measure. They looked like proclamation sent down from heaven, which indeed they might have been if God had not had a sense of humor."

An oft-told tale places Maude Adams on a platter carried onstage, aged nine months. Born in Salt Lake City to theater folk, Adams saw her New York career skyrocket after starring in 300 performances of *The Little Minister* (1897) by J. M. Barrie (1860-1937) and then essaying the title role in Barrie's *Peter Pan* (1905). Her success and popularity made her rich, but Adams was also a loner; she never married. After retiring from acting in 1918, Adams worked for years with General Electric to create a lamp good enough for indoor color photography—it was said she wanted to play Peter Pan on screen. She ran the drama program at Stephens College in Columbia, Missouri, from 1937 to 1950.

The look is sly and mischievous—one of the many sides of Francis Wilson (1854-1936), a beloved character actor. Almost universally liked by his peers, Wilson excelled in every theatrical and literary form he attempted: minstrelsy and musicals, plays and prose. His excellent memoirs provide a sense of his humor: he called the memoirs *Francis Wilson's Life of Himself,* and the byline reads, "By Himself." The work is also a long love letter to his innumerable pals and fellow players, from Edwin Booth to Annie Pixley, with whom he appeared in *M'Liss.* Wilson was the first president of Actors' Equity Association, and he led the organization when it went on strike for the first time in 1919.

It was partly her soulful-
eyed beauty, partly her
remarkable talent that
helped Julia Marlowe to
exude romance and play
the romantic heroine.
These women were
hardly melodramatic,
Pauline-tied-to-the-tracks
types, but the colossal
and titanic women of
Shakespeare. Born in
England, raised in Ohio,
Marlowe was bitten by
the theater bug quite
young and had years of
training before her 1895
Broadway debut. She
married E. H. Sothern
(1859-1933), scion of
an acting dynasty, and
together their acting
was indelible: Ophelia
and Hamlet; Beatrice
and Benedick; Juliet and
Romeo. At the height
of their careers, Sothern
and Marlowe opened
the sumptuous New
Theatre with an *Antony
and Cleopatra* (1909) that
made stage history.

Joseph Jefferson (1829-1905) came from a long line of actors; his great-grandfather worked with the great David Garrick (1717-79). Unlike his forebears however—and like James O'Neill—Jefferson was associated mostly with a single role: Rip Van Winkle, based on Washington Irving's story, although his repertoire did include many classic characters. In this photograph (ca. 1889-90), he is appearing (at right) as one of them: Bob Acres in *The Rivals* (1775), the comedy of manners by Richard Brinsley Sheridan (1751-1816), opposite Sir Lucius O'Trigger, played by W. J. Florence (1831-91). Jefferson was one of the earliest actors ever filmed—the 1896 *Awakening of Rip* is in the National Film Registry. Chicago's well-respected theater awards are named for Jefferson.

As a boy in Boston, Nat C. Goodwin discovered his mimicking abilities and set his sights on the stage. After his education, he flitted from clerkship to clerkship, giving readings and mimicking until finally he was cast in a melodrama—and fainted upon his entrance. Later attempts at acting were more successful, and he made impressions in leading New York productions, including the original *Evangeline, or, The Belle of Acadia* (1874). Adroit at Shakespeare and deft at Gilbert and Sullivan, Goodwin mastered dozens of roles. He was considered theatrical royalty at the time he produced and starred in Clyde Fitch's *Nathan Hale* (1899), which also starred his new wife, Maxine Elliott. His final Broadway role was in *Why Marry?* (1917), which won the first Pulitzer Prize in Drama.

To theatergoers at the end of the nineteenth century, Della May Fox (1871-1913) was forever known as the "Little Trooper," her title role in a now-forgotten 1894 musical. A decade earlier, the comic-opera asset had debuted in an all-children version of *HMS Pinafore,* yet she was still childlike of face and, equally perplexing to critics, completely adored by audiences. In the following years, Fox acted with Lillian Russell and comedian DeWolf Hopper (1858-1935) before succumbing, in 1900, to what the *New York Times* called "a nervous breakdown." Whereupon she married and retired, except for a brief return to the stage before her death.

As a longtime member of Augustin Daly's company, John Drew, Jr., was a pillar of the New York stage. Here, in a scene from *Christopher, Jr.* (1895), a farce by Madeleine Lucette Ryley (1859-1934), a hammer inexplicably hangs from his fingers, prompting Maude Adams, opposite, to wear one of the expectant facial expressions that made her the most exciting actress of her day.

"Give My Regards to Broadway," "Over There," "The Yankee Doodle Boy"—none of these songs were written when George M. Cohan posed for this picture. He's on the left as part of the Four Cohans, beside father Jere (1848-1917), mother Nellie (1854-1928), and sister Josie (1874-1916). Headstrong and prodigiously gifted as a singer, dancer, author, and composer, Cohan assumed responsibility for the group before turning 18. In time, the Cohans became the highest-paid family act in vaudeville, conquering New York after years shunning Manhattan's marquees. Post-vaudeville, his sister's career progressed more quickly than his, so Cohan turned to writing songs and skits that electrified Tin Pan Alley. Later, his producing partnership with Sam H. Harris (1872-1941) created enormously popular hits, including *Little Johnny Jones* (1904). Cohan was likely born on July 3, not the Fourth, despite what his "Yankee Doodle" lyric suggests. After *45 Minutes from Broadway* (1906), he was the premier musical leading man in the land, epitomizing Broadway, patriotism, and the possibilities of American music and musical theater. Cohan also starred in Eugene O'Neill's only comedy, *Ah, Wilderness!* (1933) and the musical *I'd Rather Be Right* (1937) by composer Richard Rodgers (1902-79) and Lorenz Hart (1895-1943) as president of the United States. A statue of Cohan stands in New York's Duffy Square, near Times Square. A commemorative U.S. stamp was issued in his honor in 1978.

Every good story needs an enemy. This one's name is Abraham Lincoln Erlanger (1859-1930)—A. L. to friends, trouble to the rest. Erlanger and his partner, Marc Klaw (1858-1936), opened a theatrical booking agency in the 1880s. At the time, booking networks were haphazardly organized, yet it was common and expected for actors to tour their stock companies relentlessly. So Klaw and Erlanger devised efficient procedures for booking troupes, and ultimately operated the Syndicate, a ruthless monopoly that controlled stage production for more than 20 years. Actors abhorred the Syndicate's tactics, most notably Mrs. Fiske, but its power was, for a time, unquestioned and supreme. Klaw and Erlanger were also prolific Broadway producers and theater builders: the New Amsterdam and the Erlanger (now the St. James) rose under their aegis. Their bulldog business practices also incited the 1919 actors' strike. Only their fiscal losses made them yield to the actors' demands.

J. J. Shubert (1879-1963) was one of three brothers who radically changed the American theater. He and brothers Sam S. (1878-1905) and Lee Shubert (1871-1953) were born in Eastern Europe and raised in Buffalo. As the 1800s ended, the Shuberts began running theaters all across upstate New York—as Klaw and Erlanger's Syndicate reached its zenith, with 700 theaters in its control. By 1900, Sam was in New York City leasing theaters, and soon, in New York City and elsewhere, the Shuberts posed a direct challenge to the Syndicate. After nearly 20 years, the Shuberts were victorious, owning more than 100 theaters nationwide and presenting over 500 plays and musicals. The organization, no longer run by a Shubert, is still Broadway's biggest landlord.

As New York City expanded north, so did the theaters, but it took Oscar Hammerstein I (1847-1919), grandfather of the famous lyricist, to push things up to Times Square. Back in 1900, Times was called Longacre Square, and despite the building of the Empire Theatre and other structures, it was seen as risky to build so far north. Hammerstein did, though, because he wanted to bring opera—his true love—to the masses. He built more than 10 theaters in New York City as far north as Harlem, and his opera company was the Metropolitan Opera's rival for years. A German émigré who came to the U.S. with only pocket change, Hammerstein made and lost fortunes. He is standing at 42nd Street and Broadway— the world's crossroads.

Caroline Louise Dudley (1862-1937) married Leslie Carter at 18; by 27, she'd bitterly divorced him. Mrs. Carter then approached David Belasco and asked him to teach her how to act. Belasco and Carter—who kept her ex-husband's surname to spite him—were a blockbuster team: In Belasco's *The Heart of Maryland* (1895), she swung 35 feet above the audience on the clapper of a belfry bell; her popularity grew further after Belasco's *Zaza* (1899) and *DuBarry* (1901). In 1906, Carter remarried and Belasco banished her. By the 1910s and 20s, Carter was a vaudevillian, playing minor roles in silents and Broadway plays, a relic of an old era.

Sixty years before William Wyler (1902-81) directed the Oscar-winning film starring Charlton Heston (1924-2008), this stage version of the 1880 novel *Ben-Hur* by General Lew Wallace (1827-1904) was a great success. Six times in the next 18 years some version of *Ben-Hur* would run on Broadway, the masses eating it up again and again. In part the story of Jesus, *Ben-Hur* focused on Judah, a young Jerusalem nobleman. On Broadway, Jesus was portrayed as a beam of white light. The famous chariot scene, meanwhile, was accomplished with live horses and chariots, a treadmill, and a moving cyclorama. The character of Messala, Judah's childhood friend, was originated by William S. Hart (1864-1946), later a star of silent-film westerns.

Perhaps the revue era would have thrived without the Ziegfeld Follies, but it was far richer and more glamorous for it. These chorines were part of the first Ziegfeld Follies in 1907. Many editions followed into the 1920s and beyond. Florenz Ziegfeld (1867-1932) was a character. He communicated by telegram even while sitting in a theater seeing his own shows. Caricaturist Samuel Marx (1902-92) called him "Mussolini's only rival as a publicity seeker." Marx also described Ziegfeld's favorite hobby as yachting, "while a fleet of Rolls Royces parade the shore waiting for him to tire of life on the ocean blue." As a producer, Ziegfeld most notably mounted *Sally* (1920), *Show Boat* (1927), and *Whoopee!* (1928). Later editions and film versions of the Follies were authorized by Ziegfeld's widow, Billie Burke (1885-1970), later Glinda the Good Witch in *The Wizard of Oz* (1939). Appearing in the 1907 Follies was comedienne Helen Broderick (1891-1959). Vaudeville great Nora Bayes (1880-1928)—who introduced George M. Cohan's song "Over There" years later—joined the show near the end of its run. Other Follies luminaries through the years: Eve Arden (1908-90), Fanny Brice (1891-1951), Eddie Cantor (1892-1964), Marion Davies (1897-1961), W. C. Fields (1880-1946), Marilyn Miller (1898-1936), Will Rogers (1879-1935), Barbara Stanwyck (1907-90), and Sophie Tucker (1884-1966).

The 79 performances of the *Ziegfeld Follies of 1907* played in three theaters: the Jardin de Paris (part of Oscar Hammerstein I's Olympia Theatre complex), the Liberty Theatre, and the Grand Opera House, a now-forgotten West 23rd Street venue. Of these, only the Liberty's facade is still extant. Built in 1904, the Liberty hosted Cohan's *Little Johnny Jones* (1904); a Shubert-produced, Ada Rehan–starring revival of *The Taming of the Shrew* (1905); *George White's Scandals of 1921,* one of the first shows of George Gershwin (1898-1937); and *Lady Be Good* (1924), pairing George with his lyricist brother Ira Gershwin (1896-1983). But the Liberty, pretty though it was, was hardly a distinguished house, and was converted to a movie theater in the 1930s, which it remained for more than 50 years. This photograph shows it dark in the early 1920s, its marquee advertising silent films.

55

Even beside her era's most beautiful actresses, Maxine Elliott was fetching. She arrived in New York in her teens and spent years with various acting companies, but, wrote historian Ward Morehouse (1899-1966) in his book *Matinee Tomorrow,* she "was never a brilliant actress." Rather, Elliott "was tremendously convincing in her tears, and it was always Clyde Fitch's contention that she could outsob any actress he had ever known." No wonder Fitch starred her in four of his plays. Elliott often acted with her husband, Nat C. Goodwin, including in Fitch's *Nathan Hale* (1899), which proved so profitable for him professionally. Her younger sister, actress Gertrude Elliott (1874-1950), married English actor Sir Johnston Forbes-Robertson (1853-1937). Elliott was fiscally savvy and earned great sums for her work. She became the first woman since Laura Keene (1826-73) to run a theater named for herself, a Broadway house that opened in 1908. She retired in the 1920s.

The interior of Maxine Elliott's Theatre was sumptuous and elegant, like the actress who ran it and named it for herself. Critic Sheldon Cheney (1886-1980) called its facade "perhaps the most beautiful playhouse exterior in the country. Its quiet loveliness, its perfect restfulness, its dignified sense of decorative restraint, mark it as a building conceived in just the spirit the drama should evoke in the architect." At its 1908 opening, the rumor was that the theater was a gift to Elliott from J. P. Morgan (1837-1913); she insisted Lee Shubert was her business partner. Either way, its appointments—and backstage amenities—far exceeded what actors expected. *The Children's Hour* (1934) by Lillian Hellman (1905-84) premiered here; revues and musicals by Jerome Kern (1885-1945) and Cole Porter (1891-1964) also ran here, as well as plays by John Millington Synge (1871-1909), George Bernard Shaw, Noël Coward (1899-1973), and William Somerset Maugham (1874-1965). It was a radio and TV studio before its 1960 demolition.

Broadway may be star-driven, but it's the dependable, enduring character actor who keeps things humming. Ferdinand Gottschalk was one such actor. Wrote critic Ward Morehouse in 1950, Gottschalk was "a frail, undersized actor . . . a meticulous, fussy, old-womanish Englishman with a genius for characterization. He was never a star during all of his 50-odd years on the stage and he never wanted to be. . . . It was also agreed that Ferdie Gottschalk had played with nearly all of the great ladies of the drama but that he had never embraced any of them." But Gottschalk, Morehouse added, "went his way serenely, unconcernedly, from management to management, play to play, star to star." For some people on Broadway, having a job is the best thing in the world.

One of Ferdinand Gottschalk's great stage successes was Clyde Fitch's *The Climbers* (1901), starring—and produced by—Amelia Bingham (1869-1927). Eleven years earlier, Bingham was still Amelia Swilley, waiting tables at a restaurant in a Hicksville, Ohio, hotel her father owned. There, Lloyd Bingham (1865?-1915), manager of a traveling acting troupe, spotted her, later marrying her. A few years later, Bingham made her Broadway debut, and by 1900 she'd assembled an acting company of her own, leasing the Bijou Theatre, where she produced *The Climbers,* becoming what many consider to be the first actress-producer in Broadway history. This image is from *Olympe* (1904), based on a Dumas novel.

Another actress who achieved notoriety in a Clyde Fitch play was Olga Nethersole (1863-1951). The play was *Sapho* (1900), based on a novel by Alphonse Daudet (1840-97). Historian Allen Churchill (1912-88) called her character, Fanny LeGrand, "a Camille-like lady of departed morals who was accomplished in the art of using her gleaming flesh to trap men." Jean, one such man, is taken with her, and takes her—after a scene Churchill describes as "suspiciously like an orgy"—to an offstage bedroom. This shocked the audience, and in an innovative publicity ploy, a clergyman was paid to denounce *Sapho* as the "most immoral play of modern times." Public nuisance charges were issued for Nethersole; her costar, Hamilton Revelle (1872-1958); Nethersole's manager; and the owner of Wallack's Theatre. The sensational trial ended when the jury, after 12 deliberative minutes, acquitted them all. *Sapho* played on Broadway at least five times thereafter.

Clara Bloodgood (1870-1907), wrote Ward Morehouse, "was a stage-struck New York society woman who thought she could act and went about proving it to herself and many dubious friends." Certainly Clyde Fitch thought her talented, casting her in *The Climbers* (1901), *The Way of the World* (1901), *The Girl with the Green Eyes* (1902), *The Coronet of the Duchess* (1904), and as the female lead in *The Truth* (1907), his finest play, about a married woman who compulsively lies. She was also cast in the original New York production of Shaw's *Man and Superman* (1905). Broadway reviews of *The Truth* were unkind, so it quickly went on tour. Alas for Bloodgood, it was a London hit for a rising star named Marie Tempest (1864-1942); when Fitch dedicated the published version of the play to Tempest, Bloodgood became convinced that he preferred Tempest's acting to her own. Touring with *The Truth* in Baltimore, Bloodgood, confronted by a stage manager about a pistol she'd purchased, surrendered the weapon, but promptly bought another one. Shortly before curtain time, a self-inflicted gunshot wound ended her career less than a decade after it began.

Long before becoming an icon of interior design, Elsie de Wolfe (1865-1950) was another actress who catapulted to fame on the shoulders of a Clyde Fitch play, *The Way of the World* (1901). "Since Miss de Wolfe was famous for her neighborly habit of nodding to her friends in the audience," recalled critic Brooks Atkinson, "Fitch wrote one scene in which she appeared to be riding in an automobile through Central Park. As the automobile (a very smart prop in those days) gave the illusion of puttering along, Miss de Wolfe nodded to her friends without getting out of character." For years de Wolfe was the companion of prominent theatrical agent Elizabeth Marbury (1856-1933). At 60, long past her stage career, de Wolfe "astonished everyone . . . by marrying Sir Charles Mendl (1871-1958), the worldly and charming press attaché at the British Embassy in Paris." Lady Mendl, wrote de Wolfe biographer Jane S. Smith (?-?), "was famous long after most people remembered quite why."

In her memoirs, Ethel Barrymore is typically modest. As a young girl, she wrote, "I was a shy little mortal, with large eyes cast down in continual agonizing bashfulness." Yet as niece of John Drew, Jr., daughter of Maurice Barrymore, and sister of John and Lionel, acting DNA was clearly in her genes. Her breakthrough Broadway performance was as the female lead in Clyde Fitch's *Captain Jinks of the Horse Marines* (1901); her famous profile, unyielding work ethic, and stunning talent never flagged for nearly 60 years, and her performances in Somerset Maugham's *The Constant Wife* (1926) and *The Corn Is Green* (1940) by Emlyn Williams (1905-87) were considered indelible. Barrymore became an Oscar-winner in 1944 for *None but the Lonely Heart*. The next year she acted in her last Broadway role, then pursued film. Her last role was on TV in 1957.

The Empire Theatre, built in 1893 at 40th Street and Broadway, represented the theater district's push to Times Square. Like Oscar Hammerstein I's nearby cultural palaces, producer Charles Frohman's Empire was ornate, and in its double lobby hung portraits of the day's great actors. This photograph was taken when Somerset Maugham's *Jack Straw* (1908) was at the Empire, starring Ethel Barrymore's uncle John Drew, Jr. During its 60-year existence, the Empire housed many superb New York premieres. There was *The Little Minister* (1897) and *Peter Pan* (1906) by J. M. Barrie as well as *The Barretts of Wimpole Street* (1931) by Rudolf Besier (1878-1942), and *Threepenny Opera* (1933) by Bertolt Brecht (1898-1956) and Kurt Weill (1900-1950), *Life with Father* (1939) by Howard Lindsay (1889-1968) and Russel Crouse (1893-1966), *The Member of the Wedding* (1950) by Carson McCullers (1917-67), *I Am a Camera* (1951) by John Van Druten (1901-57), and *The Time of the Cuckoo* (1952) by Arthur Laurents (1918-).

Sothern and Marlowe as romantic archenemies Beatrice and Benedick in a 1904 revival of *Much Ado About Nothing:*

BEATRICE
I had rather hear my dog bark at a crow than a man swear he loves me.

BENEDICK
God keep your ladyship still in that mind, so some gentleman or other shall scape a predestinate scratched face.

BEATRICE
Scratching could not make it worse an 'twere such a face as yours were.

BENEDICK
Well, you are a rare parrot-teacher.

BEATRICE
A bird of my tongue is better than a beast of yours.

In 1905, a coterie of wealthy, influential New Yorkers—including a Vanderbilt and an Astor—proposed building a theater for the social elite. The New Theater, opened in 1909, was perhaps Broadway's most elegant house, a colossal statement in Italian Renaissance style. Seating 3,000, it accommodated opera and drama yet lacked decent acoustics. Its first production, Sothern and Marlowe in *Antony and Cleopatra*, was a disastrous effort, setting a tone for the theater from which it never recovered. It was demolished in 1929.

Florodora (1900), which typified early twentieth century musical comedy, originated in London and ran 505 performances in its first New York run. Written by Owen Hall—the pseudonym used by theater critic James Davis (1853-1907) when writing for the stage—and songwriter Leslie Stuart (1863-1928), the paper-thin plot concerned a popular fragrance manufactured by a slick American entrepreneur in the Philippines. "Tell Me Pretty Maiden" was the hit song of the show, sung by the famous sextette of *Florodora* girls—the precursor to the Ziegfeld girl and the Radio City Rockettes—and their six "Gentle Strangers." Offstage, being a *Florodora* girl was often a ticket to marriage; scores married stage-door Johnnys during the various runs of the show. This photo is likely from the 1920 revival.

Florodora (1900) initially ran at the Casino Theatre, a heavily ornamented Moorish house on Broadway and 39th Street that was built in 1882 by Rudolph Aronson (1856-1919), who produced light operas such as *The Belle of New York* (1897) by Gustave Kerker (1857-1923), which was playing when this image was recorded in 1897. Among its illustrious tenants: *Erminie* (1886), featuring Francis Wilson, and the New York premiere of Gilbert and Sullivan's *The Yeomen of the Guard* (1888), as well as *The Chocolate Soldier* (1909), *Very Good Eddie* (1916), *Oh, Lady! Lady!* (1918), *The Vagabond King* (1925), *The Desert Song* (1926), and *The New Moon* (1929). In 1930, the growing garment district forced the theater's demolition.

Daniel Frohman (1851-1940)—brother of producer Charles and a sterling theater man in his own right—built the Lyceum Theatre in 1903. It remains Broadway's oldest surviving theater in continual use and among its most exquisite, with a beaux arts delirium of limestone, Roman columns, and marble staircases. It was designed to be self-enclosed, including scene-building and carpentry studios and wardrobe rooms. High atop the theater was Frohman's private apartment; when his wife Margaret Illington (1881-1934) overacted, he'd wave a handkerchief out a secret window no one else could see. Today the apartment houses the Shubert archives. Nearly 300 productions spanning a hundred years have played here. Key Broadway premieres included *The Lion and the Mouse* (1905) by Charles Klein (1867-1915), *Anatol* (1931) by Arthur Schnitzler (1862-1931), *The Postman Always Rings Twice* (1936) by James M. Cain (1892-1977), *Born Yesterday* (1946) by Garson Kanin (1912-99), *The Country Girl* (1950) by Clifford Odets (1906-63), *Look Back in Anger* (1957) by John Osborne (1929-94), *A Taste of Honey* (1960) by Shelagh Delaney (1939-), and *The Caretaker* (1961) by Harold Pinter (1930-). From 1965 to 1969, it was leased to the acclaimed APA-Phoenix Repertory Company; after a return to commercial productions with *Wings* (1979) by Arthur Kopit (1937-), *Master Harold . . . and the Boys* (1982) by Athol Fugard (1932-), and a self-titled solo show by Whoopi Goldberg (1955-), the National Actors Theatre founded by Tony Randall (1920-2004) played here during the 1990s. Twenty-first-century hits include *I Am My Own Wife* (2003) and *The Lieutenant of Inishmore* (2006).

Was there ever a more winsome Peter Pan than the role's originator, Maude Adams? Her 1905 performance in Barrie's play is beloved by scholars and can only be imagined by the rest of us. The *New York Times* review of the play, published November 7, 1905, likely sums it up: "Maude Adams is Peter—most ingratiatingly simple and sympathetic. True to the fairy idea, true to the child nature, lovely, sweet, and wholesome. She combines all the delicate sprightliness and the gentle, wistful pathos necessary to the role, and she is supremely in touch with the spirit of it all."

Composer Victor Herbert (1859-1924) is most closely associated with the operetta *Babes in Toyland* (1903), a direct effort to duplicate the success of the first stage version of *The Wizard of Oz*, by L. Frank Baum (1856-1919), which opened nine months earlier. "Despite its resemblance to Toyland of Oz," considered musical theater historian Cecil Smith, "the Herbert score, with its 'March of the Toys' and its adroit use of connecting and incidental music, gave *Babes in Toyland* a musical lift *The Wizard of Oz* had sorely needed." Herbert's other significant works include *The Fortune Teller* (1898), *The Red Mill* (1906), *Naughty Marietta* (1910), and *The Dream Girl* (1924).

After Victor Herbert, Franz Lehár (1870-1948) was perhaps the most gifted operetta composer of his day. His best work was arguably *The Merry Widow* (1907), derived from a now-obscure 1861 play by Henri Meilhac (1831-97)—a Frenchman who, ironically, wrote libretti for a dozen Jacques Offenbach (1819-80) operettas. Its most famous piece of music, "The Merry Widow Waltz," caused a minor sensation when the operetta opened at the New Amsterdam Theatre. There were Broadway revivals in 1921, 1929, 1931, and 1943. This photograph shows lovely Ruby Dale (?-?), a person whose back story would seem to be lost to the ages, in costume for the original New York production.

Built by Klaw and Erlanger for over a million dollars—a gargantuan sum at the time—the New Amsterdam, especially the interior, was an orgy of art nouveau ornamentation. Opened one week earlier than the 45th Street Lyceum in 1903, the theater's first tenants were unremarkable—trifling musical burlesques with titles like *Waffles* and *Looney Park.* In 1913, Florenz Ziegfeld took over; his roof-garden Midnight Frolics were staged as well as his Follies in the auditorium. Historian Mary C. Henderson (19??-) notes, "The Follies and the Frolics became the seedbeds of the greatest musical talent yet seen on the American stage." The Great Depression was unkind to the venue: from 1936 until the late 1970s it was a movie theater. Its grotesque disrepair eventually included a gaping ceiling hole that exposed its innards to the elements. In 1993, the Disney Company obtained a long-term lease on the house, with celebrated theater architect Hugh Hardy (1932-) hired to restore the New Amsterdam to its former glory. *The Lion King* reopened the house in 1997; Disney's *Mary Poppins* arrived in 2006.

THALIA THEATRE.

טהאליא טהעאטער, 46-48 בואערי.

עקסטרא!

צום ערשטען מאהל זיים יודישעט
טהעאטער עקזיסטירם

עקסטרא!

צום ערשטען מאהל זיים יודישעט
טהעאטער עקזיסטירם

מאדאם
בערטהא קאליש
אלם האמלעט

מאדאם
בערטהא קאליש
אלם האמלעט

עהרען בענעפים פאָרשטעללונ.
פיר

עהרען בענעפים פאָרשטעללונג
פיר

מאדאם בערטהא קאליש

מיטוואך אבענדס 30 יאנואר

צור אויפפאהרונג קאסם
שעקספיערם בעריהממע דראמא

☞ האמלעט ☜

מאדאם בערטהא קאליש אלם האמלעט

It's nearly dawn on June 6, 1929. Down in the Bowery, near the entrance to the Manhattan Bridge, a decrepit old theater erupts in flames. Efforts are made to put out the blaze, but the damage is done: the Thalia Theatre, also called the Bowery Theatre, is gone. Since 1826 a theater has stood here and five earlier times it burned: 1828, 1836, 1838, 1845, and 1923. Each time, repairs or rebuilding commenced, for the Thalia, its massive columns hardly white or gleaming, was one of the final links to a time when New York City's stage activities were located far downtown. Over 103 years, the Thalia hosted everything seen on the American stage: blackface performers, melodramas, Shakespeare, circus acts, minstrel shows, plays for Irish and German immigrants, Yiddish theater, vaudeville, and Eastern drama. This is a handbill in Hebrew from a 1901 production of *Hamlet.* It starred Bertha Kalish (1872-1939) and this partial translation tells the rest of the story: "Extra! Extra! For the first time in the Yiddish theater: Mme. Bertha Kalich as Hamlet. The only other woman ever to have undertaken the role of Hamlet was Sarah Bernhardt . . ."

In his book *Black Musical Theatre: From Coontown to Dreamgirls*, Allen Woll (19??-) writes that two African-American stage minstrels, Bert Williams (1874-1922) and George Walker (1873-1911), proved "white audiences would attend black shows in the city's most elegant theatres." One such show, revolutionary for its time, was *In Dahomey* (1903); this image shows a magazine article promoting the show. After charting separate paths in vaudeville, Williams and Walker formed an act, "Two Real Coons," and ended up in New York, where they appeared in several shows, including the successful *Sons of Ham* (1900). Woll notes that *In Dahomey* "revealed Williams and Walker's fascination with African themes and characters." It was also the first all-black show to play a major Broadway theater. Because of that, as the *New York Times* reported of the show's opening, "there have been times when the trouble-breeders have foreboded a race war. But all went merrily last night."

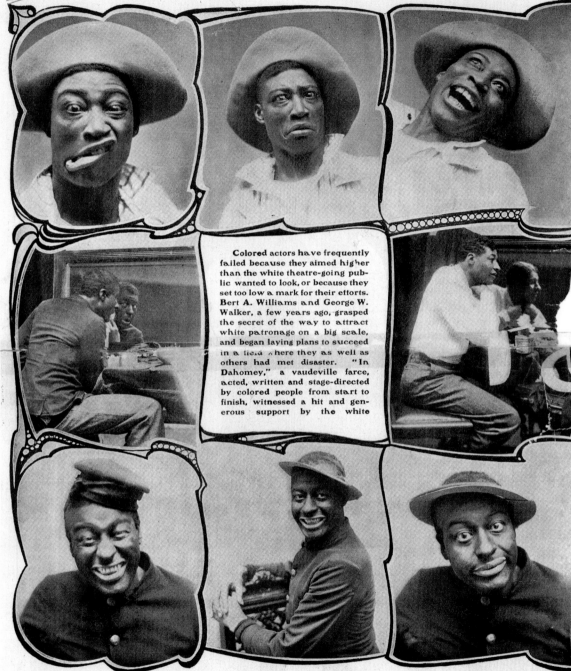

WILLIAMS AND WALKER, NATURE'S BLACK-FACE COMEDI

Colored actors have frequently failed because they aimed higher than the white theatre-going public wanted to look, or because they set too low a mark for their efforts. Bert A. Williams and George W. Walker, a few years ago, grasped the secret of the way to attract white patronage on a big scale, and began laying plans to succeed in a field where they as well as others had met disaster. "In Dahomey," a vaudeville farce, acted, written and stage-directed by colored people from start to finish, witnessed a hit and generous support by the white

This group of pictures, each of which was especially posed for The Standard and Vani published intact in any magazine. The prominence of the originals and thei The Standard and Vanity Fair is glad to give its readers the benef

LOOK FOR IT! DON'T MISS IT! "FUN IN A GALLERY" NEXT WEEK. THE MOST NOVEI

What are they looking for? *The Darling of the Gods* (1902) by David Belasco and John Luther Long (1861-1927) holds the answer. The play unfolds during the era of the Japanese "sword edict," when the emperor stripped the samurai of their weapons, and stars Blanche Bates (1873-1941) and George Arliss (1868-1946). Bates played Yo-San, daughter of the prince of Tosan, and Arliss (winner of the Oscar for Best Actor for *Disraeli* in 1930) played the minister of war. In Broadway's early days, it was common for Caucasians to play ethnic roles, an unthinkable practice today.

Blanche Bates was one of
the more popular actresses
in Belasco's stable. Born
in Oregon, she grew up in
San Francisco, debuting
there in the early 1890s.
Augustin Daly hired her
for his company in 1898,
but the arrangement
apparently failed: Having
created a major role in a
now-forgotten play called
The Great Ruby (1899),
Bates withdrew after two
performances. Her work
with Belasco was more
productive. Following *The
Darling of the Gods* (1902),
Bates created the title role
in Belasco's *The Girl of
the Golden West* (1905).
Ward Morehouse called
it "a roaring and flavorful
melodramatic piece" with
a climax that involves a
wounded outlaw, hidden in
a loft by the girl, dripping
blood upon the sheriff
pursuing him.

This rare image shows Belasco at work. The play is *The Rose of the Rancho* (1906), co-written with Richard Walton Tully (1877-1945), which tallied 240 performances in its initial run, returning to the boards twice in 1907 for another 119. Frances Starr (1886-1973), who acted under Belasco for an unprecedented 16 years, starred; he also hired her for, among other plays, the brilliant *The Easiest Way* by Eugene Walter (1874-1941) in 1909 and in revival in 1921. Here, she receives direct advice from the master. What is he saying?

This is the enduring Mrs. Fiske, looking sophisticated yet pensive as Cynthia Karslake in *The New York Idea* (1906) by Langdon Mitchell (1862-1935), a play about marriage and divorce that opened eight days before *The Rose of the Rancho* (1906). The original production marked the Broadway debut of actor-director Dudley Digges (1879-1947), who would go on to play everything from Boss Mangan in *Heartbreak House* (1920) to Mr. Zero in *The Adding Machine* (1923) to Harry Hope in *The Iceman Cometh* (1946).

Duse. Just the name connotes theatricality. But Duse—first name, Eleonora (1859-1924)—represented the apotheosis of inartificial stage acting for more than 50 years. According to biographer Arthur Symons (1865-1945), Duse was "the greatest of living actresses" because "she has a more subtle nature than any other actress" and "expresses her nature more simply. All her acting seems to come from a great depth, and to be only telling profound secrets." Duse's widely varied repertoire included Shakespeare, Henrik Ibsen, Eugène Scribe (1791-1861), Victorien Sardou (1831-1908), Pierre Corneille (1606-84), Luigi Pirandello (1867-1936), Émile Zola (1840-1902), and Maxim Gorky (1868-1936). She personally produced many of the plays of Gabrielle D'Annunzio (1864-1938), with whom Duse had a love affair, for they afforded her the chance to play a slew of memorable heroines. Born to traveling thespians, Duse died near the end of her American farewell tour, in a Pittsburgh hotel room.

TESTS, TRIALS, AND TRANSITIONS

(1910–1920)

Broadway, like much of the world, looked very different at the end of the 1910s from its appearance at the beginning. It was the effect of World War I, to be sure, but changes on the stage had already been under way. They simply became clearer as time went on.

Realism, naturalism, a sense of experimentation—these were in; hackneyed acting and writing were out. Veiller's *Within the Law* and Shaw's *Major Barbara* and *Androcles and the Lion* are but three intriguing examples of many other plays from this time. And for all of its openness to everything new, Broadway could still be completely daft. Notice the photograph in front of the Winter Garden Theatre, a procession of automobiles ready to head to a baseball game. That was Al Jolson's idea—and his favored team lost. Talk about sound and fury signifying nothing!

As they were gaining support for universal suffrage, women were gaining coinage on the stage: a portrait of the prolific Rachel Crothers is included to symbolize their rise. Actors, who found their collective voice when they went on strike in 1919, are also saluted.

In musical theater, the Ziegfeld Follies were far from everything audiences were talking about, but they certainly did predominate. And that's why, beyond a great photograph of Ziegfeld himself, his hands coolly in his pockets, a shot of Doris Eaton is included, the youngest-ever Follies girl. As of this writing, she is 104, yet young to us forever.

Also included are some breathtaking streetscapes and architectural images, such as a pen-and-ink sketch of the Eltinge Theatre. In the late 1990s, the building was hydraulically rolled down 42nd Street, its innards converted to a multiplex, its facade preserved. There's also the outside of the now-demolished Playhouse Theatre, showing dozens of doughboys. The war was "Over There," but war-weary soldiers on the home front sought reprieve at the theater.

It is said that William Gillette gave more than 1,300 performances as Sherlock Holmes over 30 years. For most actors, that would be enough success for one career. But Gillette's talents—including playwright, director, and producer—were inexhaustible. And he used his gifts to full advantage. By the time *Sherlock Holmes* opened on Broadway in late 1899, Gillette had been acting and writing for more than 20 years; he'd already had success with *Secret Service* (1896). But *Sherlock Holmes,* based on a play by Arthur Conan Doyle (1859-1930) involving his famous fictional detective, demonstrated even more profoundly Gillette's ability to become subsumed in a character. He would offer further examples in J. M. Barrie's *The Admirable Crichton* (1903) and the same playwright's *Dear Brutus* (1918), featuring 18-year-old Helen Hayes (1900-1993). In 1915 Gillette codified his acting theories in a speech, published as *The Illusion of the First Time in Acting,* and remained devoted to stage realism throughout his career. He was the first man to play Sherlock Holmes on radio and film.

Within the Law (1912), written by Bayard Veiller (1869-1943), logged 541 performances on Broadway, and scores more on the road. It's about a shopgirl unjustly jailed for theft who avenges her erstwhile employer by marrying his son. Veiller wrote the play in three months and most leading producers—like George M. Cohan and Charles Frohman—rejected it until William A. Brady (1863-1950), whose producing career entailed more than 250 shows, as well as the management of several heavyweight boxing champions, optioned it. Veiller needed cash and sold the play to Brady outright. In Chicago, after *Within the Law* received mixed reviews, Arch Selwyn (1877-1959)—a producer and brother of actor-playwright Edgar Selwyn (1875-1944)—convinced Brady to sell his interest in Veiller's play. The Selwyns then proceeded to produce it on their own and made a fortune. Later, despite having no obligation to do so, the Selwyns began paying Veiller a small salary. One day, Arch Selwyn asked Brady if he might have any other plays to sell to him. Brady responded, "Young man, it will give me a great deal of pleasure if you will get the hell out of my sight."

Within the Law (1912) opened the Eltinge Theatre on 42nd Street, where its 541-performance run was never exceeded by any other production. It was built by producer Al Woods (1870-1951) and named for Julian Eltinge (1881-1941), the legendary female impersonator who had made him a rich man. As the eighth house built on 42nd Street, it was lavishly decorated, with an Egyptian, Roman, and African-style interior, orchestra seats labeled slender, medium, and stout, and a terra cotta exterior. When Woods went bankrupt during the Great Depression, the Eltinge became a burlesque house; in 1942, it became a movie house called the Empire, remaining so for many years. As part of the 42nd Street redevelopment efforts, the theater was lifted off its foundation in 1998 and gently rolled down the block. Its gutted interior became a multiplex, but today the beautifully fenestrated facade remains pristine.

George Bernard Shaw's plays are so firmly a part of the Western canon that it's hard to imagine their American premieres. Each was memorable, and the stories behind the first Broadway mountings of *Arms and the Man* (1894), *The Devil's Disciple* (1897), *Candida* (1903), *Man and Superman* (1905), the once-banned *Mrs. Warren's Profession* (1905), *Caesar and Cleopatra* (1906), and *Pygmalion* (1914) could fill a separate book. *Androcles and the Lion* (1915), Shaw's take on the tale of a runaway Roman slave, was brought to Broadway by Harley Granville-Barker (1877-1946), Shaw's acolyte and talented actor-writer-director friend, in repertory with a production of *A Midsummer Night's Dream* that was highly innovative.

Lewis Waller (1860-1915) was an Englishman who sailed the Atlantic to conquer Broadway. Known as a romantic lead, his takes on Shakespeare enhanced his reputation—including his Brutus in *Julius Caesar,* Faulkenbridge in *King John,* and title role in *Henry V.* In 1912 and 1913, Waller toured America and may have regretted speaking to the press. "It is perfectly evident," he told the *New York Times,* "that New York, generally speaking, does not want good plays or heavy plays or even good comedies. What New York wants is light musical comedy or sensational drama that will take the place of moving pictures. If they don't get that, they will take moving pictures." Maybe he was unhappy with the *Times'* October 1912 review of *Henry V.* Its critic wrote, "If there is to be abundant scenery and many costumes, it is at least pardonable to ask that these things shall be fresh and clean, that the former shall be so lighted and handled that an effective atmosphere is created and preserved, and that the latter shall be so worn as to intensify rather than disturb illusion." Presumably Waller was much happier back home.

Three shows ran at the Winter Garden Theatre during most of 1912: *Sesostra, The Whirl of Society,* and *A Night with the Pierrots.* None are memorable, but this image recalls a great Broadway story. The latter show starred Al Jolson (1886-1950), the incomparable singer and showman. He'd risen to stardom the year before and now had the press following his every move. So on May 24, 1912, Jolson took the entire Winter Garden company—each performer, musician, crew member, and all their families—to see a baseball game, the New York Highlanders (now the New York Yankees) versus the Washington Senators. Jolson was so confident that the Senators would triumph, the group not only occupied at least 20 automobiles, but a brass band in the front car led their procession. New York won.

The name J. Hartley Manners (1870-1928) sounds contrived; perhaps he'd be forgotten entirely today if his wife had not been Laurette Taylor (1884-1946), a stage legend of whom dissertations are still being written. Her last role was as Amanda Wingfield in *The Glass Menagerie* (1945) by Tennessee Williams (1911-83); it was the perfect bookend for a career that soared stratospherically with *Peg o' My Heart* (1912), which Manners wrote and directed. The play is sweet—a young woman sporting the "wrong" accent finds herself in a proper upper-crust English household, where the challenge is to transform her into one of them. The play ran for 604 performances, setting all kinds of records. Films and popular songs have kept Peg in the public eye for nearly 100 years. This photograph depicts a rare item—the program from the final performance of the original Broadway run, in 1914.

Peg o' My Heart (1912) was the first production at the Cort Theatre, one of Broadway's few extant houses east of Seventh Avenue. John Cort (1861-1929) was a West Coast–based impresario who hoped he'd improve his fortunes by establishing a Broadway outpost; the Shuberts took over the theater in 1927. Designed by Thomas Lamb (1871-1942), the marble exterior features Corinthian columns and plasterwork; the Pavanozza marble interior sports a proscenium arch with art glass once capable of illumination. The Cort was long viewed as a lucky house. Ethel Barrymore, Lillian Gish (1893-1993), Ruth Gordon (1896-1985), Laurence Olivier (1907-89), Marlon Brando (1924-2004), Katharine Hepburn (1907-2003), Uta Hagen (1919-2004), Grace Kelly (1929-82), and Jane Fonda (1937-) all played here, often in hits. Broadway premieres included *A Bell for Adano* (1944) by Paul Osborn (1901-88), *The Shrike* (1952) by Joseph Kramm (1907-91), *The Rainmaker* (1954) by N. Richard Nash (1913-2000), *The Diary of Anne Frank* (1955) by Frances Goodrich (1890-1984) and Albert Hackett (1900-1995), *Sunrise at Campobello* (1958) by Dore Schary (1905-80), *Purlie Victorious* (1961) by Ossie Davis (1917-2005), *Home* (1980) by Samm-Art Williams (1946-), and *Ma Rainey's Black Bottom* (1984) by August Wilson (1945-2005). In 1974, *The Magic Show* began a 1,920-performance, four-and-a-half-year run. In 1995, a revival of *The Heiress* (1947) by Ruth Goetz (1912-2001) and Augustus Goetz (1901-57) confirmed Cherry Jones (1956-) as one of the nation's foremost actresses. *The 39 Steps,* a parody of Hitchcock's famous film, was transferred by the Roundabout Theatre Company from Broadway's American Airlines Theatre to the Cort in April 2008, marking the 245th production in the house.

Here is Florenz Ziegfeld in the 1910s, at the height of his Broadway fame. Did any stage impresario ever look so secure?

Broadway in the 1910s, wrote historian Allen Churchill, cavorted "madly to music that was a mixture of Negro ragtime and hints of jazz-to-come." That spirit was evident in 1911, when producer Lew Fields presented a musical fluff ball, *The Hen-Pecks.* It featured a "stringy, insouciant dancer-comedian" named Vernon Castle (1887-1918). "English-born, loose-limbed and blithely debonair, Vernon had recently shattered feminine hearts by marrying Irene Foote, a flower of New Rochelle society." Vernon and Irene Castle (1893-1969) won fame first in Paris, introducing the Turkey Trot, Bunny Hug, Grizzly Bear, and other syncopated steps. In 1912, they returned to the U.S., succeeded on stage and film, wrote a how-to dance book, and conquered vaudeville. Their fame was such that the Castles also ran a nightclub, a dancing school, and a restaurant, Sans Souci. Their Broadway apogee came with *Watch Your Step* (1914), the first of 21 musicals fully scored by Irving Berlin (1888-1989), for which this photograph was taken. Vernon was a World War I pilot, killed when his plane crashed during flight maneuvers in Texas.

Watch Your Step (1914) also starred short, baby-faced Frank Tinney (1878-1940), a blackface comic who eschewed "black" dialect and apparently had an awful temper. For several years he'd had an adulterous relationship with a beautiful Ziegfeld Follies chorine, Imogene "Bubbles" Wilson, later film star Mary Nolan (1905-48). When Tinney caught her canoodling with another man, he beat her sufficiently for her to call the police. A subsequent trial ended Tinney's marriage, but Wilson refused to testify against him. Around this time, Wilson also announced she was leaving Broadway to make movies. All of which horrified Ziegfeld, and this *Time* magazine article tells the rest: "The greedy newspapers, swollen with the story, alarmed the finical Florenz. He wired his press agent to keep Imogene out of the newspapers. . . . Mr. Tinney sailed for Europe. Imogene visited him on the steamer. *Variety* concluded that they must be reconciled since they spent several hours in his stateroom apparently in earnest conference. The newspapers bulged anew. Imogene went back to the Follies and found herself without a job."

Not that female playwrights were absent from Broadway, but Rachel Crothers (1878-1958) was a one-person drama factory, with 24 plays produced between 1906 and 1937, mostly directed by the author. As the dean of American female dramatists—Susan Glaspell (1876-1948) was another—Crothers was a social-change agent, playing indispensable roles in the theater's relief efforts during the world wars and serving as a model for several generations of women both on and off the stage. Her best plays include *A Man's World* (1910), *He and She* (1920), and *Susan and God* (1937); the latter holds up especially well today. In a 1941 *New York Times Magazine* interview, Crothers said, "I've been told that my plays are a long procession reflecting the changing attitudes of the world toward women. If they are, that was completely unconscious on my part. Any change like that, that gets on the stage, has already happened in life."

This Broadway marquee was gigantic and visually commanding. It is advertising the Winter Garden Theatre's *Passing Show of 1915*, the second Broadway show for the legendary Marilyn Miller.

Born in Indiana, Marilyn Miller debuted on stage at age four; she helped put her family's vaudeville act, the Five Columbians, on the map. Lee Shubert discovered Miller at a London club, and beginning with appearances in the *Passing Show of 1914* and the *Passing Show of 1915*, her career took off. In 1918, Ziegfeld placed Miller in that year's Follies, where her ability to act, tap, sing, and play opposite Eddie Cantor, W. C. Fields, and Will Rogers made her an immediate audience favorite.

After starring in *Sally* (1920), a revival of *Peter Pan* (1924), and *Sunny* (1925), she was Broadway's highest-paid star. After a dispiriting Hollywood sojourn, Miller returned to Broadway with the musical *As Thousands Cheer* (1933) by Moss Hart (1904-61) and Irving Berlin. Now Miller was suffering from chronic ailments, including sinus infections and alcoholism. She died after sinus surgery, and more than 2,000 people attended her funeral.

Born Mariam Edez Adelaida Leventon, the life of Alla Nazimova (1879-1945) took her from Yalta, Russia, her birthplace, to Moscow Art Theatre of Konstantin Stanislavski (1863-1938) to Broadway, where she debuted in Henrik Ibsen's *Hedda Gabler,* signing a contract without being fluent in English. In her many Broadway roles—in the plays of Ibsen, Anton Chekhov (1860-1904), and especially in *Mourning Becomes Electra* (1931) by Eugene O'Neill—she was billed simply as Nazimova. She enjoyed a major Hollywood career (her L.A. estate was called "the Garden of Allah"), including a Camille some consider superior to that of Greta Garbo (1905-90), and a scandalous Salome. This photograph was taken in 1928 when Nazimova played Madame Ranevsky in Chekhov's *The Cherry Orchard,* part of Eva Le Gallienne's ascendant Civic Repertory Theatre. Nazimova was also the godmother of former First Lady Nancy Reagan (1921-).

So important was Nazimova to Broadway's box-office that when the Shuberts were opening a new theater in 1910, they named it for her. Located on 39th Street between Sixth and Seventh avenues, the venue lasted just 16 years; after Nazimova left the Shuberts' management in 1911, they simply stripped her name off the building. Few memorable shows had premieres here, but its elegant exterior and intimate interior made it ideal for straight plays. This photograph was shot in 1926, shortly before its demolition, the marquee advertising a show running elsewhere in town.

Six weeks of the 10 months that *Very Good Eddie* (1915) played on Broadway, it ran at the 39th Street Theatre. The show, one of several intimate musical efforts of the time, featured a rollicking book by Philip Bartholomae (1879-1947) and Guy Bolton (1884-1979), lyrics by a slew of song-scribblers, and music by rising composer Jerome Kern. Its plot was wacky—about a very short man married to a very tall woman and a very tall man married to a very short woman, and what ensues following an inadvertent partner swap. Audiences cared little, having surely been diverted by minor characters like Always Innit, Gay Anne Giddy, and Lily Pond. *Very Good Eddie* was co-produced by veteran agent Elizabeth Marbury, hence Elsie de Wolfe's enlistment to design the set. A 1975 Broadway revival earned three Tony nominations.

Unlike his slick producer brother Arch Selwyn, Edgar Selwyn took a torturous path to theatrical prominence. As recounted in his play *Rolling Stones* (1915), the Alabama-born Selwyn went to Chicago at 17 to make his fortune. The opposite occurred: flat broke, he threw himself off a bridge into the Chicago River, landing on ice instead of water. After he climbed despondently back to terra firma, a gunman accosted him and said, "Your money or your life!" Selwyn's reply—"My life"—stunned the gunman. Shortly after, the gunman and the would-be dead man went to a pawnshop together, splitting the proceeds from the sale of the gun. Those funds helped Selwyn restart his life and brought him to New York, where he sold neckties, stage managed, played small and large roles, and wrote such plays as *The Arab* (1912), which established his reputation. At his death, Selwyn had been a fixture in theater—an actor, playwright, producer, and play broker—for 40 years; the All-Star Feature Films Corporation, which he founded with his brother, helped create the Goldwyn Pictures Corporation, a forerunner of MGM.

Like many of George Bernard Shaw's socially provocative plays, *Major Barbara* (1915) created a stir—in this case, owing to its sharp criticism of the Salvation Army. Grace George (1879-1961), one of the more daring and versatile actresses of her day, played the key role of Barbara Undershaft in the original Broadway production—on the right is Ernest Lawford (1870-1940) as Adolphus Cusins, Barbara's fiancé. The play ran in repertory with such plays as Langdon Mitchell's *The New York Idea* (1906), *The Liars* (1898) by Henry Arthur Jones (1851-1929), and Shaw's own *Captain Brasshound's Conversion* (1907). The original New York run of *Major Barbara,* incidentally, marked one of the first Broadway performances by Guthrie McClintic (1893-1961) in the role of a butler. McClintic would later marry actress Katharine Cornell (1893-1974) and become a famous director in his own right.

With fewer than 900 seats, the Playhouse Theatre was an intimate house. Its restrained design—compared with other Broadway venues being built at the time—suggested it might make an ideal home for the evolving American drama, which it did. Opened in 1911 and used as a legitimate house except for three years as a radio station, the Playhouse hosted the original New York productions of Shaw's *Major Barbara* (1915), *The Show Off* (1924) by George Kelly (1887-1974), *Street Scene* (1929) by Elmer Rice, Tennessee Williams' *The Glass Menagerie* (1945), *In the Summer House* (1953) by Jane Bowles (1917-73), and *The Miracle Worker* (1959) by William Gibson (1914-). Both the interior and exterior can be seen in the film *The Producers* (1968) by Mel Brooks (1926-); the building was demolished the following year. This photograph was taken in September 1918 when *She Walked in Her Sleep*—a long-forgotten play by George Broadhurst (1866-1952), for whom the Broadhurst Theatre is named—was running. Notice the scores of World War I doughboys.

The musicals of the 1910s may have been short on substance, but they never lacked for ageless melodies. *Oh, Lady! Lady!* (1918) was another period effort featuring music by Jerome Kern, with Guy Bolton and P. G. Wodehouse (1881-1975) co-authoring book and lyrics. Kern, of course, became one of Broadway's chief innovators, while attempting to count up the various musical efforts that Bolton and Wodehouse contributed to is to tempt mathematical fate. In *Oh, Lady! Lady!*, there is a disapproval. There are also necessary subplots: the boy's friend trying to court the boy's former fiancée, as well as gangsters and a bohemian party in Greenwich Village. Vivienne Segal (1897-1992) played the girl (Molly Farringdon) and Carl Randall (1898-1965) played the boy (Willoughby Finch). Segal later achieved immortality as Vera Simpson in the musical *Pal Joey* (1940) while Randall became a noted choreographer. In 1918, they made a pretty cute couple, didn't they?

So much myth surrounds Broadway lore that it's easy to forget that rags-to-riches dreams do come true. For 30 years, Frank Bacon (1864-1922) was a road actor, making a living but not a great one in the days when actors' working conditions were poor. Indeed, Bacon was a Hollywood bit player when he was cast in *The Fortune Hunter* (1909) by Winchell Smith (1872-1933)—on tour. Upon meeting producer John Golden (1874-1955), Bacon mentioned having penned a play himself, called *A House Divided.* Smith read it, rewrote it, and in 1918 Golden produced it under the new title *Lightnin'.* With Bacon playing Lightnin' Bill Jones, a sagely sort who tells tall tales, the play ran 1,291 performances, the longest run of a Broadway play up to that time. In 1919, when Actors' Equity went on strike against producers, Bacon shook hands with Golden in his dressing room and promptly hired a stagecoach, riding it around Manhattan emblazoned with the words "*Lightnin'* has struck!" Bacon played *Lightnin'* for years, forever beloved by his fellow players.

This is Doris Eaton (1904-) around 1920. At 16, she had already become the youngest-ever Ziegfeld girl (she fudged her age) and was now a principal in the Ziegfeld Follies, which was also employing her siblings in memorable sketches and songs. In the 1920s, Eaton starred in revues and comedies on Broadway and in Los Angeles, where her film career flourished. From the 1930s to the 1960s, she worked for and owned various Arthur Murray Dance Studio franchises, then began to run a ranch in Norman, Oklahoma. Doris Eaton Travis today is the last living Ziegfeld girl. In 1998, she returned to Broadway— to the New Amsterdam Theatre, where she first performed in 1918—to take part in the Easter Bonnet charity competition held by Broadway Cares/ Equity Fights AIDS. Travis' appearance at the annual event became its highlight. In 2004, at age 100, she led a conga line on the New Amsterdam stage. *Century Girl* by Lauren Redniss (197?-) is a tribute to a genuine performing legend.

Of the 1919 actors' strike, critic Brooks Atkinson wrote, "There can never have been another strike that entertained the public so exuberantly." When the union struck on August 6, scores of shows closed and actors set up shop anywhere they could—even the street—to explain themselves to the masses. Over the next month, benefits for the union at the Lexington Avenue Opera House made for high entertainment—the talk of the town. And through it all, actors stressed the need to end ghastly practices like long unpaid rehearsal periods, closing road plays and stiffing actors of return fares, and making actors pay for costumes. Not everyone was pro-union—George M. Cohan created the Actors Fidelity Union in protest—but it all proved costly: producers lost millions. Today, Actors' Equity remains the chief representative of American stage actors.

With the 1920s looming, a new generation was in the wings. Second from left is Alfred Lunt. Milwaukee-born, schooled in Wisconsin and Boston's Emerson College, here he's in his first starring role on Broadway in *Clarence* (1919) by Booth Tarkington (1869-1946), playing the titular hapless war hero. At left is Helen Hayes, a young "first lady of the American theatre." The other woman is Mary Boland (1880-1965), a veteran of a dozen-odd Broadway shows, later a major Hollywood character actor. During *Clarence*'s run, Lunt met a British woman, Lynn Fontanne, who would earn her first leading role in *Dulcy* (1921) by George S. Kaufman (1889-1961) and Marc Connelly (1890-1980).

The Lunts, as they were known, went on to become the greatest acting team of the twentieth century.

George Bernard Shaw's *Heartbreak House* (1920) was the first of 18 plays by the great Irish dramatist produced on Broadway by the Theatre Guild, which was formed in 1919 to introduce plays and musicals of significance and consequence onto the American stage, with commercial concerns a secondary, not a primary, concern. Over the next half-century, the Guild would produce more than 200 Broadway shows, ranging from the plays of Eugene O'Neill to *Oklahoma!* (1943) and other landmark musicals. *Heartbreak House* marked the first Broadway show directed by Dudley Digges; the actor's powerful intellect and matchless access to emotionalism seemed to dovetail beautifully with a play about England in the last throes of moral authoritativeness. Albert Perry (1870-1933) played crusty, eccentric, endearing and increasingly disillusioned Captain Shotover. Elizabeth Risdon (1888-1958) plays Ellie Dunn, who marries for money, being unable to marry the man she loves. This causes her to utter a famous Shavian line: "If I can't have love, that's no reason why I should have poverty."

THE ROAR OF THE POSTWAR GREASEPAINT

(1920–1930)

From Shaw's *Heartbreak House* to Eugene O'Neill's first flowering with such plays as *Beyond the Horizon* and *The Emperor Jones,* Broadway in the 1920s was venturing to places that would have been unthinkable a decade or two earlier. Experimental works—Sophie Treadwell's *Machinal,* Elmer Rice's *The Adding Machine,* Karel Čapek's *R.U.R.*—were offered to audiences who sometimes, though not always, were eager for new theatrical possibilities. It was the heady and giddy era following World War I, and musical comedy was very much in on the action as well, with the rise of the Gershwins, of Rodgers and Hart, of Kern and Hammerstein, of Porter. On the rise, too, were theater buildings—the Guild Theatre, for example, symbolizing the call to greatness issued by the Theatre Guild and confirmed by its remarkable selection of new plays to produce.

As hems on skirts rose, so did the curtain on reconceived classics: notice the sketch for the set of John Barrymore's *Richard III,* or the photograph of Barrymore in his landmark *Hamlet.* A few old-timers were going with the flow of Broadway's evolution—like Owen Davis, the cigar in his mouth and gruff mien belying the more than 200 plays he wrote in his lifetime. Favorites here are the photo of the audience at the one-year anniversary performance of George Kelly's *The Show Off,* and the one representing the Moscow Art Theatre's first visit to the U.S., which would have a pivotal influence on the craft of acting.

That 1920s Broadway roared like the decade itself is an understatement: at the midpoint of the decade, more than 200 productions were opening annually, over 260 in 1928 alone. In perspective, that's equal to six or seven seasons of Broadway openings today. For this reason, this chapter—and the next one, on the 1930s—feature more images than any other. It was a time of monumental theatrical fertility. The world will wait long for the curtain to rise on an encore.

Eugene O'Neill won the first of four Pulitzer Prizes for *Beyond the Horizon* (1920), a three-act tale that bears some similarities to the shattering, towering plays that would ensure his fame. In New England, the Mayo family has a mother, a father, and two sons—one, a dreamer anxious to find what lies "beyond the horizon"; one destined, it seems, to till the land to preserve the family legacy. When the love of one of the brothers for a woman intervenes, however, the brothers' fates unexpectedly switch, leading to tragic consequences for all. This photograph is from the 1926 revival of the play.

Beyond the Horizon (1920) played the Morosco Theatre, one of Broadway's most elegant, intimate houses. Designed by architect Herbert J. Krapp (1883-1973), it was built by the Shuberts for manager, producer, director, and writer Oliver Morosco (1876-1945), who helped the Shuberts destroy the monopolistic Syndicate. Opened in 1917, it was a warhorse, hosting such original productions as George Kelly's *Craig's Wife* (1925), *Our Town* (1938) by Thornton Wilder (1897-1975), Noël Coward's *Blithe Spirit* (1941), John Van Druten's *The Voice of the Turtle* (1943), *Death of a Salesman* (1949) by Arthur Miller (1915-2005), Tennessee Williams' *Cat on a Hot Tin Roof* (1955), *The Visit* (1958) by Friedrich Duerrenmatt (1921-90), Arthur Miller's *The Price* (1968), *Butley* (1972) by Simon Gray (1936-), *The Shadow Box* (1977) by Michael Cristofer (1945-), the revue *Side by Side by Sondheim* (1978), and *Da* (1978) by Hugh Leonard (1926-). The drama surrounding the 1982 demolition of the Morosco Theatre, the Helen Hayes Theatre, and the Bijou Theatre is widely deemed one of the saddest episodes in the history of the American stage, a dereliction of moral duty on the part of theater owners and elected officials of the time. Occupying the site today is the Marriott Marquis hotel, a monument to the postmodern fascination with concrete.

As noted, Marilyn Miller was already a box-office attraction when she starred in the musical *Sally* (1920). But Florenz Ziegfeld's production—for which Jerome Kern and Victor Herbert collaborated on music—catapulted her heavenward after she sang "Look for the Silver Lining." Apparently a triumph of imagination over talent: "Her performance of the song provided an instance of the extent to which the public hears what it wants to, when it is enamored of a performer," wrote Cecil Smith. "Miss Miller possessed a wiry little voice, sometimes hardly audible, except for a single enormous tone of F . . . which threw the whole song out of scale. . . . With *Sally*, Marilyn Miller became the dearest love of the musical-comedy audience of the 1920s." This image shows another *Sally* star—Leon Errol (1881-1951), who later starred opposite Lupe Velez (1908-44) on film—and six peachy chorines.

While O'Neill won his first Pulitzer for *Beyond the Horizon* (1920), it was *The Emperor Jones* (1920) that solidified the dramatist as a master of stagecraft. Using expressionism and a soupçon of realism, *The Emperor Jones* finds Brutus Jones, a convicted African-American murderer, escaping prison to a Caribbean island and styling himself a king. Mostly a monodrama (only the first and last scenes involve dialogue), the play proved an overnight hit for the Provincetown Players, moving from Greenwich Village to the Selwyn Theatre—O'Neill's second Broadway production of 1920. Charles S. Gilpin (1878-1930), whose resume included scores of odd jobs including stints in vaudeville and minstrelsy, played Brutus; *The Emperor Jones* had one of the first racially integrated casts in American theater history. Gilpin played Brutus several more times during the 1920s, but fell from O'Neill's favor when he began changing words and drinking too much. Still, his place in theatrical history is assured.

The acculturation of all-white Broadway accelerated with the musical *Shuffle Along* (1921), which ran nearly 500 performances at the 63rd Street Music Hall, north of Times Square. "Broadway had not seen a successful all-black show in years," noted Allen Woll, "and theatre managers argued that ticket buyers would stay away in droves. The composers and cast were virtual unknowns. . . . Word from the road was also bleak, as the *Shuffle Along* company left a well-marked trail of unpaid bills as it moved from city to city. It arrived in New York City . . . almost $18,000 in debt." Yet the music by Eubie Blake (1887-1983) and lyrics by Noble Sissle (1889-1975) sizzled and the all-black musical became a popular Broadway attraction. The objectionable practice of black actors donning blackface—as this production shot indicates—was still de rigueur as the 1920s began. Beyond the title song, *Shuffle Along*'s most memorable tune—"(I'm Just) Wild About Harry"—will be part of the American songbook forever.

After his astonishing *Richard III* (1920), John Barrymore ascended into the pantheon of theatrical greatness. Indeed, his performance in *Hamlet* (1922), designed by Robert Edmond Jones (1887-1954), was a signal event, spoken of reverentially for years after its occurrence. He is pictured here opposite John S. O'Brien (18??-1923) as Polonius. Not only was Barrymore's spontaneous, riveting Dane seen as equaling or exceeding in quality that of the legendary Edwin Booth, but Barrymore became the second actor to break an unwritten rule and play the role 101 times—one more than Booth. (An obscure actor named John E. Kellerd, 1862-1929, did it first in 1912). This *Hamlet* was Barrymore's last work on Broadway for 17 years: Hollywood became the recipient of his immeasurable talent and libidinous and reckless alcoholic personality. The likes of such talent will not be seen again.

Katharine Cornell enjoyed the kind of career actors can no longer seriously contemplate. She was utterly devoted to the stage, particularly to serious dramas, many directed by her husband, Guthrie McClintic. As Brooks Atkinson recalled, "Something psychological happened when she made an entrance. Audiences can not be indifferent to her presence. Although she was not pretty, she was beautiful—dark eyes, dark hair, a somber, patient voice, and a slightly withdrawn personality. It was as if she could not quite let go. . . . She was not spectacular, but she was electric." She debuted on Broadway in *Bushido* (1916) by Takeda Izumo (1691-1756), and the 1920s found Cornell exuding potential—especially in such plays as *A Bill of Divorcement* (1921). In the 1930s and beyond, Cornell fulfilled that potential, setting new standards for excellence on the Great White Way. This image is from McClintic's production of *The Age of Innocence* (1928), based on the novel by Edith Wharton (1862-1937).

The play *R.U.R.* (1922), which stands for Rossom's Universal Robots, singularly illustrates the multidimensional, elastic drama that found receptive audiences in 1920s Broadway, especially when the Theatre Guild was producing it. Written by Karel Čapek, a Czech playwright and a pioneer of science fiction, *R.U.R.* is a trenchant satire set in the main office of a company where mechanized creatures (Čapek credited his brother Josef with coining the word "robot") rebel against management and lay waste to civilization. Alas for them, the robots then realize they have acquired human characteristics.

Rain (1922), an adaptation of W. Somerset Maugham's short story "Miss Thompson" by John Colton (1886-1946) and Clemence Randolph (?-?), is set on the island of Pago Pago, but that was the least exotic facet of a play that started Broadway's tongues a-wagging. Jeanne Eagels (1890-1929) put in more than 900 performances as a saucy heart-of-gold prostitute whose soul a reverend is trying to save—he kills himself upon realizing his feelings for her. "In her prostitute's business casual of black-belted white dress, lace mantilla and woolen scarf, five-and-dime beads topped by a feathery hat overlooking high-button spats, sporting an umbrella, and slipping from brusque and feisty to soothed and radiant within ten seconds," wrote historian and critic Ethan Mordden (1947-), "Eagels gave Sadie the dizzy magic of the drug addict." And the audience gave Eagels the "ovation of the century" on opening night.

Consider the output of playwright Owen Davis (1874-1956) this way: Shakespeare wrote roughly 38 plays; Davis wrote five times as many—possibly as many as 300—in his 50-year career. According to the Internet Broadway Database, Davis had 10 plays open in 1906 and 11 in 1907, virtually all claptrap potboilers, many written overnight in the breathless and slapdash, melodramatic style enduringly popular as the twentieth century began. The superbly educated Davis, even so, had the wherewithal to devise dramas in tune with his times, hence his *Icebound* (1923), a Pulitzer Prize winner.

Coming just a year after *R.U.R., The Adding Machine* (1923) was Elmer Rice's turn to brutally satirize the mechanization of industry. Indeed, Rice's take on the plight of the working man is all about unrelieved agony: After 25 years as a bookkeeper, Mr. Zero (in a memorable performance by Dudley Digges) is terminated, replaced by adding machines. Having toiled for years with neither a raise nor a promotion, this is the last straw, and he murders his boss. He is tried, convicted, and executed, and is quickly found segueing from afterlife to afterlife, only to be sent back to mortality to start all over again. This image illustrates the possibilities of expressionism, experimental at the time.

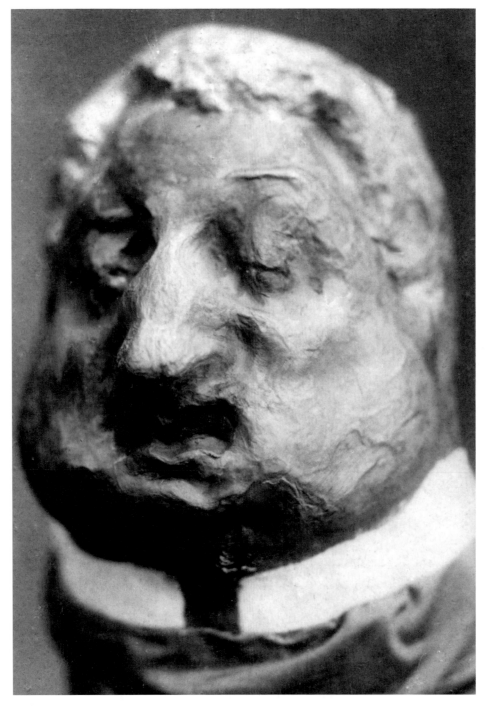

If the Moscow Art Theatre hadn't embarked on a trip to North America in 1922 and 1923, perhaps the course of American acting would have been different. But it did come stateside, commencing performances at Jolson's 59th Street Theatre of *The Brothers Karamazov, The Cherry Orchard, The Lower Depths,* and other plays in repertory, prodding American actors, writers, and directors into a decades-long study of Konstantin Stanislavsky's rich, soulful, immensely attractive productions and performances. It was especially influential upon Lee Strasberg (1901-82), who transformed Stanislavsky's methodology into the Method, founding the world-renowned Actor's Studio. The Moscow Art Theatre returned to Broadway later in 1923 and again in 1924. This image—evocative, haunting, curious—is a mask made by Russian sculptor and master photographer Nikolai Andreev (1873-1932) and now held in the collection of the Moscow Art Theatre Museum. The mask, one should note, is a representation of Youzhin, the preferred sobriquet of an actor-playwright named Prince Alexander Ivanovich Sumbatoff (?-?).

World War I may have been "the war to end all wars," but its effect upon the theater and literature were felt well into the 1920s. The rhetorically and provocatively titled *What Price Glory?* (1924) by Maxwell Anderson (1888-1959) and Laurence Stallings (1894-1968) was unyieldingly realistic yet equally romantic. This image—of actors George Tobias (1901-80, who played Abner Kravitz on TV's *Bewitched*), Fuller Mellish, Jr. (1895-1930), and Brian Donlevy (1901-72)—reflects the play's ability to echo the language and disturbing attitudes of soldiering. *What Price Glory?* centered, however, on Captain Flagg, played by Louis Wolheim (1880-1931), and First Sergeant Quirt, played by William Boyd (later William "Stage" Boyd, 1889-1935), and their tug-of-war over a woman—and how each was willing to set aside the dispute when the time came to bathe once more in the grisliness of war. Controversial and commanding, the play allowed Anderson to move from journalist to full-time playwright, becoming one of the nation's most accomplished dramatists. The question mark at the end of the title was added after the play was written.

Except for a man and woman committing suicide, all the characters in the proto-existentialist *Outward Bound* (1923) by Sutton Vane (1888-1963) are dead—and on a ship headed for the afterlife, to be judged and categorized accordingly. Not the sunniest idea for a drama, but the play was nevertheless enthusiastically received—owing in part to a cast that included Dudley Digges, Margalo Gillmore (1897-1986), and Alfred Lunt.

Designed by Herbert J. Krapp and opened in 1917—and featuring Adamsesque details in homage to the Booth and Shubert theaters nearby—the Plymouth was renamed for Gerald Schoenfeld (1924-), longtime chairman of the Shubert Organization, in 2005. For years it was run by director-producer Arthur Hopkins (1878-1950), under whose aegis many great plays were offered—not just *What Price Glory?* (1924), but Eugene O'Neill's *The Hairy Ape* (1922), *Machinal* (1928) by Sophie Treadwell (1885-1970), *Holiday* (1928) by Philip Barry (1896-1949), Elmer Rice's *Counsellor-at-Law* (1931), Rachel Crothers' *Susan and God* (1937), *Abe Lincoln in Illinois* (1938) by Robert E. Sherwood (1896-1955), Thornton Wilder's *The Skin of Our Teeth* (1942), and Noël Coward's *Present Laughter* (1946). After Hopkins' death, the Shuberts presented *The Caine Mutiny Court-Martial* (1954) by Herman Wouk (1915-); *The Odd Couple* (1965), *The Star-Spangled Girl* (1966), and *Plaza Suite* (1968) by Neil Simon (1927-); *Twigs* (1972) by George Furth (1932-); *Equus* (1974) by Peter Shaffer (1926-); the Royal Shakespeare Company's *The Life and Adventures of Nicholas Nickleby* (1981); *Plenty* (1983) by David Hare (1947-); *The Real Thing* (1984) by Tom Stoppard (1937-); *Burn This* (1987) by Lanford Wilson (1937-); *The Heidi Chronicles* (1989) by Wendy Wasserstein (1950-2006); *Dancing at Lughnasa* (1991) by Brian Friel (1929-); the musical *Passion* (1994) by Stephen Sondheim (1930-) and James Lapine (1949-); and the musical *Jekyll & Hyde* (1997) by Frank Wildhorn (1958?-) and Leslie Bricusse (1931-); among others. It remains a choice Broadway house.

George S. Kaufman and Marc Connelly, having had hits with *Dulcy* (1921) and *Merton of the Movies* (1922) and misses with *To the Ladies* (1922), *The '49ers* (1922), *Helen of Troy, New York* (1923), and *The Deep Tangled Wildwood* (1923), came roaring back with the wildly imaginative *Beggar on Horseback* (1924). At once a parable, a parody of expressionism, and a bit of theatrical genius, the play considered the fate of a poor composer urged by all around him—including his true love—to marry the daughter of a very wealthy man. While asleep, he imagines how life will be, from a wedding bouquet made of banknotes to earning millions doing nothing at a "widget" factory. Finally, the man murders them all and is tried for his crimes; his defense takes the form of a romantic ballet. Foreshadowing? Well, perhaps—the man wakes up and finds his true love ready to wed him at last. *Beggar on Horseback* was revived in 1925 and by Lincoln Center Theater in 1970. Broadway awaits its rediscovery.

Oo-Oo-Oo-Oo, Oo-Oo-Oo-Oo
When I'm calling you
Oo-Oo-Oo-Oo, Oo-Oo-Oo-Oo
Will you answer too?
Oo-Oo-Oo-Oo, Oo-Oo-Oo-Oo

"Indian Love Call" was among the memorable elements of *Rose-Marie,* an immensely successful 1924 musical that logged 557 performances at the Imperial Theatre, later becoming a summer stock favorite. The music for that song and others was written by the Prague-born Rudolf Friml (1879-1972), who'd studied with Anton Dvorak before arriving stateside in 1903; other songs were credited to Herbert P. Stothart (1885-1949), who later earned fame as the in-house musical director and composer at MGM. Friml's other theatrical composing efforts, all influenced deeply by the European operetta tradition, included *The Firefly* (1912), *The Vagabond King* (1925), and *The Three Musketeers* (1928). For *Rose-Marie,* about a woman's romance with a Canadian Mountie and, in a novel idea for the time, involving murder as a major plot point, credit for book and lyrics was shared by Otto Harbach (1873-1963) and Oscar Hammerstein II (1895-1960); the latter would achieve immortality collaborating with Jerome Kern on *Show Boat* (1927) and many musicals with Richard Rodgers. Pictured in the title role is Mary Ellis (1897-2003), who excelled in the genres of opera, musical theater, and straight plays and headlined the London stage for decades.

The Imperial has earned its name by housing musical smashes: From this now-removed stage door, the likes of Gertrude Lawrence (1898-1952), Ray Bolger (1904-87), Mary Martin (1913-90), Ethel Merman (1908-84), Zero Mostel (1915-77), Ben Vereen (1946-), and Hugh Jackman (1968-) have come and gone. And though it was for musicals that Herbert J. Krapp designed the Shuberts' 50th house, plays—Kaufman and Hart's *You Can't Take It with You* (1938), Neil Simon's *Chapter Two* (1977)—have succeeded here, too. Musical premieres include *Rose-Marie* (1924), *Oh, Kay!* (1926), *The Desert Song* (1927), *Of Thee I Sing* (1931), *On Your Toes* (1936), *One Touch of Venus* (1943), *Annie Get Your Gun* (1946), *Call Me Madam* (1950), *The Most Happy Fella* (1956), *Oliver!* (1963), *Fiddler on the Roof* (1964), *Pippin* (1972), *They're Playing Our Song* (1979), *Dreamgirls* (1981), *The Mystery of Edwin Drood* (1985), *Jerome Robbins' Broadway* (1989), and *The Boy from Oz* (2003). *Les Misérables* (1987), which premiered at the Broadway, ran here for 13 years. *Billy Elliot* (2008), based on the hit film, promises to be the next long-term tenant.

As composer Rudolf Friml caused musical excitement with *Rose-Marie* (1924) and *The Vagabond King* (1925), Sigmund Romberg (1887-1951) joined the battle with *The Student Prince* (1924), with book and lyrics by Dorothy Donnelly (1880-1928). Based on the play *Alt-Heidelberg* by Wilhelm Meyer-Förster (1862-1934), it is about a prince who disguises himself at a new school, where he falls in love with Kathie, a woman that he, being royalty, can never wed. If anything, the show was a bigger hit than *Rose-Marie,* logging 608 performances at Jolson's 59th Street Theatre. Pictured is Howard Marsh (?-1969), the lovelorn titular prince. The show's most famous song was the lilting, emotional "Deep in My Heart Dear."

In 1956, when the musical *The Most Happy Fella* triumphantly opened on Broadway, the play by Sidney Howard (1891-1939) it's based on, *They Knew What They Wanted* (1925), began its long fade from the limelight, despite having won the Pulitzer Prize. Indeed, while the musical took some plotting liberties, the play is more straightforward: it examines a woman caught between an attractive man who may or may not be good, and a good man—a heavily accented Italian immigrant—who is all but attractive. Like Howard's *Ned McCobb's Daughter* (1926) and *The Silver Cord* (1926), the play was mounted by the Theatre Guild, now universally considered a matchless purveyor of quality drama. Pictured in the role of the aging immigrant Tony is actor Richard Bennett (1872-1944). *They Knew What They Wanted* also starred Pauline Lord (1890-1950) as Amy, the anguished damsel, and Glenn Anders (1890-1981) as Tony's handsome rival, Joe.

Another Guild effort was *The Guardsman* (1925) by Ferenc Molnár, which marked the first of the legendary performances of Lunt and Fontanne (they had acted in J. Hartley Manners' *Sweet Nell of Old Drury* [1922], but not opposite each other). It was the dislike for *The Guardsman* on the part of actor Joseph Schildkraut (1895-1964)—he preferred playing Richard III instead—that permitted the pairing. Its premise may have been creaky—when an actress weary of her actor-husband seems ready to spurn him, he dresses as a guardsman and seduces her—but the acting was unparalleled. The 1931 film version was one of the Lunts' few appearances on screen.

Julius (1890-1977), Leonard (1886-1961), Arthur (1888-1964), and Herbert (1901-79)—also known as Groucho, Chico, Harpo, and Zeppo Marx—need no introduction. Their major Broadway hits—*The Cocoanuts* (1925) and *Animal Crackers* (1928)—were hilarious comic concoctions that drove George S. Kaufman, who wrote *The Cocoanuts'* book alone, and the *Animal Crackers* book with Morrie Ryskind (1895-1985) . . . well, nuts. Wrote Brooks Atkinson, "While *The Cocoanuts* was being beaten into shape on the road, [composer-lyricist Irving] Berlin unwillingly agreed to cut some of his songs, one of which was 'Always,' one of the best ballads he ever wrote. Nothing could withstand these freewheeling zanies. The writers complained that the Marxes paid less and less attention to the lines as the show went on. 'I may be wrong,' Kaufman said acidly when he once revisited *The Cocoanuts,* 'but I think I just heard one of the original lines.'"

"Never criticize a bootlegger's English if his Scotch is all right." That line—penned by writer P. G. Wodehouse—was the kind of quip that made *Oh, Kay!* (1926) a sparkling musical comedy. Another reason: songs by George and Ira Gershwin, such as "Someone to Watch Over Me," "Fidgety Feet," and "Do, Do, Do." Yet another reason: the first appearance by a pert transplanted English gal, Gertrude Lawrence, in a book musical. And yet another: a story about rum-running and bootlegging, with the obligatory dashes of mistaken identities and romance rolled out expertly by Wodehouse and Guy Bolton.

A typical fluff-ball 1920s musical comedy, *No, No, Nanette* (1925) was forgettable, despite chipper music by Vincent Youmans (1898-1946), the peppy lyrics of Irving Caesar (1895-1996) and Otto Harbach, and a fleeting book by Harbach and Frank Mandel (1884-1958). But in 1971, at the apex of what journalist Don Dunn (19??-) called "a tidal wave of Nostalgia," *No, No, Nanette* rode back to Broadway on a crest of yearning for the Jazz Era, and sporting all the casting accoutrements of old-time Hollywood, from *42nd Street* star Ruby Keeler (1910-93), whose last Broadway show was in 1929, to comedienne Patsy Kelly (1910-81), last on the Great White Way in 1932. More stunning, the production was supervised—kindly put—by Busby Berkeley (1895-1976), the master choreographer of movie musicals. Dunn's *The Making of "No, No, Nanette"* reveals the bloody innards of that revival, focusing on the innocuousness of and rivalry between its principal producers. By reintroducing the public to songs like "Tea for Two" and "I Want to Be Happy," however, this little fluff ball ran 861 performances—the original ran 321—winning four Tonys.

Eva Le Gallienne resisted a career marrying great theater with commercial success. Her dream, articulated throughout her life, was to create a repertory theater, an American version of the envied European model. She had first won audiences' hearts as Julie in *Liliom* (1921), the Molnár play upon which the musical *Carousel* (1945) was based. However, her heart was with Ibsen, Chekhov, Shaw, Barrie, Molière (1622-73)—as well as Shakespeare, and a take on *Alice in Wonderland* she utterly delighted in. Independent spirited (she lived openly as a lesbian), Le Gallienne opened Civic Repertory Theatre in 1926 at 14th Street and Sixth Avenue. Long called the Fourteenth Street Theatre, it had stood already for 60 years, back when Union Square was the northern tip of New York's Rialto; now the same site was 30 blocks south of Broadway. Stage artists admired Le Gallienne's high-minded literary and theatrical sense, and until Depression-era economics ruined it all, audiences paid $.50 to $1.50 to see the great plays of the Western canon. Civic Rep was four years gone when Berenice Abbott shot this photo on July 2, 1936. The venue was demolished two years later.

What's more Broadway than a play called *Broadway* (1926)? Except that co-authors George Abbott (1887-1995) and Philip Dunning (1890-1968) had it in mind to depict nightclub life realistically, with all the gangsters and gunfighting—over a girl, naturally— imaginable at the height of Prohibition. For Abbott, the play's 603 performances constituted yet another hit in a 70-year career that had too many of them to count. Abbott's obituary in the *New York Times* counted 113 Broadway and road shows, and recycled the 1954 assertion by journalist Gilbert Millstein (1915-99) that "on the basis of sheer frightening volume alone . . . no living individual, or possibly even dead, has contributed more to the Broadway theatre in the capacities of actor, director, producer, co-producer, author, co-author and play doctor, than George Abbott." This photo finds star Lee Tracy (1898-1968) amid a gaggle of ogle-worthy chorines.

Composer Richard Rodgers (at center) and lyricist Lorenz Hart (at right)—given a nifty script by Herbert Fields (at left)—made *A Connecticut Yankee* (1927), adapted from Mark Twain's classic tale, a rollicking time. William Gaxton (1893-1963) played the titular hero; dances were by Busby Berkeley. Classic songs include "My Heart Stood Still" and a ditty in the vernacular, "Thou Swell":

Thou swell! Thou witty! Thou sweet! Thou grand!
Wouldst kiss me pretty? Wouldst hold my hand?

At the time of *A Connecticut Yankee*, Rodgers and Hart had been collaborating for a decade or so, and wrote a fleet of songs and scores during the 1920s, *Yankee* arguably the most sophisticated. After a Hollywood detour, they returned in the 1930s, writing brilliant scores for *On Your Toes* (1936), *Babes in Arms* (1937), and *Pal Joey* (1940), among others. The alcoholic Hart died tragically. Rodgers went on to collaborate with Oscar Hammerstein II.

Something unusual occurred at the John Golden Theatre, as this wide-angle shot indicates. It was Eugene O'Neill's *Strange Interlude* (1928); the actress onstage was Lynn Fontanne. Nina Leeds' tragic, twisted life story needed nine acts and five hours to unfold, partly because the playwright, who'd spent the 1920s experimenting with dramatic form and content, expanded his efforts by having each character inform, underscore, and comment on the play's events through astonishing asides. The play began in the late afternoon and continued into the evening, with an intermission-cum-dinner break. Audiences were untroubled by such conventions: they were enraptured by the Theatre Guild's production and Fontanne's cauterizing acting. It ran 426 performances, earning O'Neill the second of four Pulitzer Prizes.

Few Broadway theaters opened with a smash hit, but the Alvin did with the musical *Funny Face* (1927). It occasioned the return of brother and sister Fred (1899-1987) and Adele Astaire (1896-1981) to the stage, and sported many great Gershwin tunes, including the title song, "High Hat," "'S Wonderful," "Let's Kiss and Make Up," and "He Loves and She Loves." The Alvin has housed more than 120 plays and musicals, and many hits: *Mister Roberts* (1948) played all its 1,157 performances here; *Annie* (1977) began its 2,377-performance run here; and *Hairspray* (2002) has logged more than 2,300 performances in the house as of this writing. Other premieres included *Girl Crazy* (1930), *Anything Goes* (1934), *Porgy and Bess* (1935), *The Boys from Syracuse* (1938), *There Shall Be No Night* (1940), *Lady in the Dark* (1941), *A Tree Grows in Brooklyn* (1951), *A Funny Thing Happened on the Way to the Forum* (1962), *Rosencrantz and Guildenstern Are Dead* (1967), *Company* (1970), *Brighton Beach Memoirs* (1983), and *Biloxi Blues* (1985). It became the Neil Simon Theatre in 1983. Designed by Herbert J. Krapp—this image is a sketch of his final design—the Alvin's name came from producers [Al]ex Aarons (1890-1943) and [Vin]ton Freedley (1892-1969). Its red-brick facade, double-height arched windows, and black-marble lobby are more distinctive than baroque.

Though best known for starring in horror flicks, Bela Lugosi (1882-1956) was no stranger to the stage. Born, appropriately, near Transylvania, he first became the most acclaimed Hungarian actor of his day, then was America-bound, where he supposedly memorized his part in Broadway's *The Red Poppy* (1922) phonetically. By 1927, Hamilton Deane (?-1958) and John L. Balderston (1899-1954) cast him in their stage version of *Dracula* by Bram Stoker (1847-1912), which Lugosi played for eight months on Broadway and two years on tour. His casting in the Hollywood film *Dracula* (1931) might be surmised a no-brainer, but legend has it that Lugosi campaigned for the job, and that the death of screen star Lon Chaney (1883-1930) sealed the deal. This menacing headshot of Lugosi was taken in 1947, more than 10 years after his last appearance on Broadway in the forgettable musical comedy *Murder at the Vanities* (1934).

Florenz Ziegfeld's production of *Show Boat*
(1927), with music by Jerome Kern and book
and lyrics by Oscar Hammerstein II, has been
examined exhaustively by musical theater
scholars. Perhaps more than any before it,
it daringly advanced the parameters and the
possibilities of American musicals as it aimed
to integrate music, narrative, and dance. Its
score—including "Bill," with lyrics by P. G.
Wodehouse—remains Kern's most glorious
and lush. This set of caricatures is from a
playbill dated September 29, 1928, nine
months into its 528-performance run. Here's
the opening of the lyric to "Ol' Man River":

Dere's an ol' man called de Mississippi,
Dat's de ol' man dat I'd like to be,
What does he care if de world's got troubles?
What does he care if de land ain't free?

On the "Cotton Blossom."

Norma Terris.

Sammy White. "Frank"

Eva Puck. "Ellie"

Norma as Terris "Magnolia."

Jules Bledsoe singing "Old Man River"

1.9.2.8.

No actress exceeded the richness of Helen Hayes, who made good material great and great material indescribable. Hayes first acted at age 5 in a school production of *A Midsummer Night's Dream;* as a teenager, her impersonation of a Ziegfeld Follies chorine persuaded Lew Fields to make her a star. Hayes' career was first controlled by producer George Tyler (1868-1946), who also sought control over her personal life. After Hayes broke with him, she could finally pull the roles of a lifetime—notably Queen Victoria in *Victoria Regina* (1935) by Laurence Housman (1867-1959), in which Hayes played Victoria from youth to old age. She was one of only nine people to win an Oscar, Tony, Emmy, and Grammy. This image is from *Coquette* (1927) by George Abbott and Ann Preston (later Ann Preston Bridgers, 1891-1967). Hayes played a woman in love with a man that her father, a doctor, despised and shot, claiming defense of his daughter's honor. Alas, Coquette carries the man's child—and commits suicide.

Helen Hayes met Charles MacArthur (1895-1956), erstwhile newspaperman. While Hayes starred in *Coquette* (1927), MacArthur and collaborator Ben Hecht (1894-1964) readied *The Front Page* (1928) for Broadway. MacArthur and Hayes were in love, but as Brooks Atkinson wrote, "He did not want to marry a woman who earned a great deal more than he did." In addition, as Hayes was Catholic, she knew her church "would not recognize her marriage to a divorced man." And so, as Atkinson relates, "Since the success or failure of *The Front Page* would be a crucial factor in her marriage to MacArthur, Jed Harris [1900-1979], producer of *Coquette,* closed it for the night when *The Front Page* opened. She sat in the balcony. The authors huddled on the fire escape. At the end of each act, Miss Hayes reported how she thought it was going. After the last act, the prolonged excitement in the theatre convinced everyone that *The Front Page* would be a hit. MacArthur proposed to Miss Hayes that night."

The play occurs in the press room of the Chicago Criminal Courts building on the day a murderer will hang; the comic tale weaves blackmail, romance, and high-velocity journalistic chatter. Standing: Osgood Perkins (1892-1937), father of film star Anthony Perkins (1932-92), as Walter Burns. Sitting: Lee Tracy, who'd starred in George Kelly's *The Show Off* (1924), as Hildy Johnson.

Born Israel Iskowitz, Eddie Cantor endured a hardscrabble Lower East Side youth, and used a mix of guts, soul, heart, and sheer talent to rise to the top. Raised by his grandmother in poverty, he learned how to entertain in the street—juggling for coins, making jokes to steer clear of gangs. In his teens he worked in vaudeville; after being cast in the *Ziegfeld Follies of 1917* and other shows, he became a star. Ziegfeld's production of *Whoopee!* (1928), based on Owen Davis' *The Nervous Wreck* (1923), made him rich, and although he lost his fortune in the 1929 crash, he conquered radio and film, becoming one of the beloved entertainers of his generation. The most famous song from *Whoopee!* goes a little like this:

Another bride, another June,
Another sunny honeymoon,
Another season, another reason,
For making whoopee.

Taken in 1935, this photo shows the Times Square Theatre, which opened in 1920, having succumbed to film, perhaps the briefest lifespan for any Broadway house. Its most famous tenants were *The Front Page* (1928), *Strike Up the Band* (1930), and *Private Lives* (1931). Architect Eugene DeRosa (1894-1942), at the behest of producers Arch and Edgar Selwyn, created a facade uniting the venue with its next-door neighbor, the Selwyn. Its silver, green, and black color scheme was unusual then as now, to say nothing of black carpeting, yet its neoclassical frontage makes the exterior one of Broadway's most august structures. Nearly 75 years after it closed as a legitimate theater, the Times Square awaits reinvention. From the 1930s until the 1990s, it showed films, closing in 1997 as part of the 42nd Street redevelopment efforts, when it was turned over to the production organization Livent, whose bankruptcy delayed its regeneration yet again. It remains standing, landmark protected, glaringly empty.

That is, indeed, Clark Gable (1901-60) in Sophie Treadwell's *Machinal* (1928), his Broadway debut. While loosely based on the crime of Ruth Snyder (1895-1928) and Judd Gray (1892-1928), lovers who conspired to murder Snyder's husband, Treadwell elected not to use melodrama to explore the story, but to take a cue from the expressionist experimentalists of the era, such as O'Neill and Rice, and make a larger statement about women's battle against patriarchy. The woman is Zita Johann (1904-93), who earned rave reviews for her work. She was married to actor John Houseman (1902-88) from 1929 to 1933, during which time she made several Hollywood films, including playing the love interest of Boris Karloff (1887-1969) in *The Mummy* (1932).

While Sophie Treadwell drew inspiration from Elmer Rice for her expressionistic *Machinal* (1928), Rice was thinking of *Street Scene* (1929), which won the Pulitzer Prize. The play—some 60 characters—occurs in front of a Manhattan brownstone. The stories of the street's inhabitants were shocking only insofar as they were realistic; indeed, what was shocking was Rice's vision of depicting the everyday dramas of everyday folks. *Street Scene* marked an early triumph for set designer Jo Mielziner (1901-76), who'd amass 200 Broadway credits as a set and lighting designer, including the original production of Shaw's *Saint Joan* (1923), *A Streetcar Named Desire* (1947), *Death of a Salesman* (1949), *Guys and Dolls* (1950), *The King and I* (1951), *Picnic* (1953), and *Gypsy* (1959). Mielziner won 9 Tonys and was nominated for 23.

Another memorable Hollywood figure to begin in the theater was Preston Sturges (1898-1959). Long before his films *The Great McGinty* (1940), *Sullivan's Travels* (1941), and *Hail the Conquering Hero* (1944), Sturges, scion of a prominent Chicago family, and connected to the performing arts through his mother's friendship with dancer Isadora Duncan (1877-1927), styled himself an actor-playwright. After debuting on Broadway as an actor in Paul Osborn's now-forgotten *Hotbed* (1928), he was inspired to write *The Guinea Pig* (1929) by what one woman said while rejecting him. The play's reviews encouraged Sturges to write *Strictly Dishonorable* (1929, pictured), which was a smash. The plot is loony—about a New Jersey couple in a Manhattan speakeasy run by an Italian immigrant, where an opera singer sets his sights on the unhappily wedded wife—but the dialogue crackled, and the play ran 321 performances. Unfortunately, all of Sturges' subsequent Broadway efforts were flops. The theater's loss became filmdom's gain.

Porgy (1927), a play by Dorothy (1890-1961) and DuBose Heyward (1885-1940), was another sublime achievement for the Theatre Guild. It marked not only the authors' first Broadway effort but the directorial debut of Rouben Mamoulian (1897-1987), whose exquisite technique enabled him to tackle such other landmark works as the Gershwins' opera *Porgy and Bess* (1935), Rodgers and Hammerstein's *Oklahoma!* (1943) and *Carousel* (1945), and the Kurt Weill–Maxwell Anderson musical *Lost in the Stars* (1949). Frank Wilson (1885-1956) was the original Porgy; Evelyn Ellis (1894-1958), the original Bess. Pictured are Jack Carter (1902-67, as Crown) and other members of the *Porgy* company. It ran 367 performances at the Guild Theatre.

The Guild Theatre's Moorish design lends enlightenment to any production. It opened in 1925 with a revival of Shaw's *Caesar and Cleopatra,* featuring Helen Hayes as the female lead; besides *Porgy* (1927), premieres during the Theatre Guild years included *Marco Millions* (1928), *Elizabeth the Queen* (1930), *Mourning Becomes Electra,* and *Ah, Wilderness!* (1933). When the Guild concluded its house no longer suited its needs, it leased it for radio broadcasts. In 1950, the American National Theatre and Academy (ANTA) purchased it and owned it for more than 30 years; productions then included many revivals and such premieres as *J.B.* (1958), *A Man for All Seasons* (1961), *No Place to Be Somebody* (1969), and *Bubbling Brown Sugar* (1976). In 1981, Jujamcyn Theaters bought the theater; James H. Binger (1916-2004), the company's chairman, renamed it for his wife Virginia (1916-2002), a lifelong theater fan. With such shows as *City of Angels* (1989), *Jelly's Last Jam* (1992), *Smokey Joe's Café* (1995), and *Jersey Boys* (2005), it is known as a hit house. It was renamed for playwright August Wilson in 2005. This image shows a Guild-era view of the interior lobby.

SING ME A SONG OF SOCIAL STUDIES

(1930–1940)

Theater scholars and sociologists can make what they wish of the inverse relationship between the poverty of the Depression-era 1930s and the richness of Broadway—that it was a superb era is the emphasis here. Among comedies, nothing was better than the convulsively funny plays of George S. Kaufman and Moss Hart, hence the photographs of *Once in a Lifetime* and *The Man Who Came to Dinner* that bookend this chapter. Yet perhaps that is unfair to the incomparable Noël Coward, represented here with *Private Lives* and *Design for Living,* the latter a gorgeous image in which Coward luxuriates between Alfred Lunt and Lynn Fontanne.

The Lunts occupy a special place in this volume. Indeed, there are more images of them than anyone else. For they were more than remarkable—they symbolized the apogee of theatrical brilliance. Look at images of *Amphitryon 38* and *Idiot's Delight,* and dare disagree.

Some of this chapter's streetscapes are jaw-dropping. Examine what flanked the Ethel Barrymore Theatre long before there was a parking lot on one side, a bank skyscraper on the other. Follow that with the spellbinding interior of the Longacre.

And then segue through to the musicals and the dramas: Included are *Girl Crazy* (featuring a young Ethel Merman), *The Band Wagon* (featuring the still-young Astaires), and several genuine surprises. Also here are Helen Hayes in *Victoria Regina,* Katharine Cornell in *The Barretts of Wimpole Street,* and Lynn Fontanne yet again, now in *Elizabeth the Queen.* See plays by Hellman, Saroyan, and Barry—and faces of Bankhead, Kelly, and Hepburn.

This chapter also remembers the vast social changes wrought by the Great Depression. The portrait of a boyish Orson Welles is a find. Who were those people protesting the end of the Federal Theatre Project? And what of Elia Kazan, fists raised upward, in Clifford Odets' *Waiting for Lefty?* Yes, brother, we can spare a dime.

Before it was a Talking Heads song, *Once in Lifetime* (1930) was a play by George S. Kaufman and Moss Hart. The story behind the play's creation climaxes Hart's autobiography *Act One*. Raised poor, Hart's stage exploits had until now come to little, but one day after the play's rave reviews, Hart moved his whole family from their dreary tenement for a better life. "I could see a long double line of people extending the full length of the lobby from the box-office," Hart wrote. "The line spilled out under the marquee where another line was patiently forming under umbrellas. I got out of the cab and walked into the lobby and stood gaping at all the people. . . . The box office man, looking up for a moment to glance across the lobby, caught sight of me and smiled. There is no smile as bright as the smile of a box-office man the morning after a hit." Pictured, left to right, are Grant Mills (189?-1973) as Jerry Hyland, Jean Dixon (1896-1981) as May Daniels, and Hugh O'Connell (1898-1943) as George Lewis. The play concerns three vaudevillians heading west, suspecting that talkies are the wave of the future; only the daffy George is successful. Kaufman created the role of struggling screenwriter Lawrence Vail, who cracks under the pressure of no work; later in the 406-performance run, Hart briefly replaced him.

Nearly 10 years before Moss Hart's life turned from rags to riches with the opening of *Once in a Lifetime* (1930), Irving Berlin reached yet one more pinnacle when the Music Box Theatre opened in 1921. Producer Sam H. Harris had approached Berlin about writing a revue, promising to find a house for the show. Instead, Harris built the theater especially for the annual *Music Box Revue* (1921-24). Harris' widow, in 1941, sold half the shares in the theater to Berlin and half to the Shuberts, who had already begun amassing an interest in the building. And that's how it stood until 2007, when the Berlin estate sold its shares to the Shubert Organization, which now owns it outright. With its sweeping columns, the facade seems formidable, but the neo-Georgian interior is a symphony of elegance. Major premieres: *Dinner at Eight* (1932), *Stage Door* (1936), *I Remember Mama* (1944), *Picnic* (1953), *Bus Stop* (1955), *Five Finger Exercise* (1959), *Any Wednesday* (1964), *Sleuth* (1970), *Deathtrap* (1978), *Agnes of God* (1982), *A Few Good Men* (1989), *Closer* (1999), *The Vertical Hour* (2006), and *August: Osage County* (2008).

She was born Ethel Zimmerman in Astoria, Queens, across the East River from Manhattan. As Ethel Merman (accounts vary as to when she dropped the "Zim"), she rose from being a secretary to a vaudeville player to a Broadway star very quickly, taking a role in the Gershwin musical *Girl Crazy* (1930, pictured) at age 22, singing a little ditty called "I Got Rhythm." Over the next 40 years, she headlined more than a dozen Broadway tuners, including five by Cole Porter, virtually all of them hits. She was, as the *New York Times*' obituary stated, "a chunky, aggressive star with [a] clarion voice, brash personality, shrewd comic sense and steel nerves." At the piano is Al Siegel (1899-1981), Merman's coach and famous accompanist in his own right. Merman always denied Siegel's claims that it was he who made her a star.

Another young Broadway player was Imogene Coca (1908-2001). Here she is not quite 22, appearing in the *Garrick Gaieties* (1930), the last of the three revues under that name mounted by the Theatre Guild. Unlike the first two, this one had no score by Rodgers and Hart but songs by a virtual conga line of writers, including composers Marc Blitzstein (1905-64) and Vernon Duke (1903-69), and lyricists Ira Gershwin and E. Y. "Yip" Harburg (1896-1981). Coca appeared in several more Broadway revues—*New Faces of 1934, New Faces of 1936, The Straw Hat Revue* (1939)—before taking off for Hollywood and achieving lasting fame as the sidekick of Sid Caesar (1922-) on TV's *Your Show of Shows* (1950-54). Coca returned to Broadway in the 1978 musical *On the Twentieth Century,* earning a Tony nomination.

Lynn Fontanne made a galvanizing (and middle-aged) sixteenth-century monarch in Maxwell Anderson's blank-verse play *Elizabeth the Queen* (1930); Alfred Lunt, naturally, played opposite her as the politically ambitious and maddening romantic interest, Lord Essex. It was just one of a series of Anderson plays exploring the Tudor period; *Mary of Scotland* (1936) and *Anne of the Thousand Days* (1948) were two others. Starring Bette Davis (1908-89) and Errol Flynn (1909-59), *Elizabeth the Queen* was filmed by Hollywood, released as *The Private Lives of Elizabeth and Essex* (1939).

The Band Wagon (1931) was the last Broadway show featuring both Fred and Adele Astaire. It was one memorable send-off—what Cecil Smith called "one of the most perfect revues in the history of Broadway." Sporting songs by composer Arthur Schwartz (1900-1984) and lyricist Howard Dietz (1896-1983), including "Hoops" and "Dancing in the Dark," and a book by ever-ubiquitous George S. Kaufman and Dietz, it also starred Frank Morgan (1890-1949), who later played the title role in *The Wizard of Oz* (1939), and comic gem Helen Broderick (1891-1959). Smith felt that "the delight of *The Band Wagon* lay in its transmutation of stage machinery into something approaching lyric poetry. The first American revue to take full cognizance of the revolving stage, it had two of them, and used them in all sorts of imaginative ways. . . . The Astaires danced on them as they revolved; in the first act finale the turntables turned in opposite directions as the entire cast waved from a merry-go-round."

Katharine Cornell was never absent from the Broadway scene for very long. Produced by Cornell and directed, as usual, by husband Guthrie McClintic, Cornell and Brian Aherne (1902-86) were said to be electrifying in Rudolf Besier's *The Barretts of Wimpole Street* (1931), which told the story of the meeting and romance that arose between poets Robert Browning (1812-89) and Elizabeth Barrett (1806-61), running 376 performances and later made into a 1934 film with Norma Shearer (1900-1983) and Fredric March (1897-1975). Flush, the name of the famous dog in the play and film, really was called Flush.

You're my silver lining,
You're my sky of blue;
There's a love light shining
All because of you.

With a score by George and Ira Gershwin and a book by George S. Kaufman, now paired with Morrie Ryskind, *Of Thee I Sing* (1931) was a trenchant and genuinely hilarious satire of American politics, coming just at the moment that the Great Depression seemed to deepen, and when Broadway audiences wanted to laugh. The first musical comedy to win the Pulitzer Prize, *Of Thee I Sing* follows what happens after John P. Wintergreen wins the presidency on a platform of love—resulting in a beauty contest being held for Miss White House and the winner setting off a series of events threatening to derail the Wintergreen Administration. With Vice President Throttlebottom desperately looking for something, anything, to do, things spin wildly and wonderfully out of control.

152

Private Lives (1931) wasn't Noël Coward's first Broadway play—that was *The Vortex* (1925)—but it established him as the prince of a certain kind of witty comedic sophistication. It is about a divorced couple, Amanda and Elyot, who have both remarried and, just by chance, book themselves adjacent suites in the same hotel in which to spend their honeymoons. Amanda and Elyot, of course, still care quite completely for each other. Coward wrote the play for the woman at left, Gertrude Lawrence, and he played opposite her on Broadway as well as originally in the West End. A third figure, not in the photo, is significant—Laurence Olivier, not quite 24, played Amanda's new husband, in what was his second Broadway show. Arguably Coward's best play, it has had six Broadway revivals—in 1948, 1969, 1975, 1983, 1992, and 2002.

Playwright Paul Green (1894-1981), who won the Pulitzer Prize for *In Abraham's Bosom* (1927), had *The House of Connelly* (1931) produced as the first Broadway effort by the Group Theatre, formed by Lee Strasberg, Cheryl Crawford (1902-86), who co-directed, and director-critic Harold Clurman (1901-80). Green startled Broadway with his dramas of the American South; *The House of Connelly* depicts a proud, decadent, aristocratic southern family in a new era. It had a short run, just 71 performances, but it was the result of an effort to do theater differently, "to go away to some country place with 28 actors and rehearse two plays till they were ready for production in New York," as Clurman recalled. Green's play arrived on the Group Theatre's docket when the Theatre Guild released its rights to produce it, giving the Group Theatre $1,000 toward its effort. It featured the new company's paramount actors: Stella Adler (1901-92), Phoebe Brand (1907-2004), Morris Carnovsky (1897-1992), Clifford Odets, and Franchot Tone (1905-68).

Martin Beck (1867-1940) came to the U.S. with a German acting troupe. After various odd jobs, he got involved with San Francisco's Orpheum Theater, running it by 1905. He kick-started the career of Harry Houdini (1874-1926) and in 1913 built Broadway's legendary Palace Theatre, the epicenter of the vaudeville world. When the Orpheum circuit went public in 1923, he lost his job, opening his eponymous venue the next year. Renamed for beloved caricaturist Al Hirschfeld (1903-2003) in 2003, the theater houses both plays and musicals. Key premieres: *The House of Connelly* (1931), *High Tor* (1937), *Cabin in the Sky* (1940), *The Iceman Cometh* (1946), *The Rose Tattoo* (1951), *The Crucible* (1953), *Candide* (1956), *Bye Bye Birdie* (1960), *Marat/Sade* (1965), *A Delicate Balance* (1966), *Into the Woods* (1987), and *Moon Over Buffalo* (1995). Beside its Moorish design, it's one of the few Broadway theaters with a box office opening directly on the street. This rehearsal photo shows actors, the director, stagehands, and technicians, and was taken near the top of the proscenium arch, showing a giant turret used as part of the set for the Theatre Guild's *Roar China* (1930), not one of its finer efforts.

Like Eugene O'Neill's *Strange Interlude,* which not only innovated drama but tested audiences' endurance, *Mourning Becomes Electra* was a marathon. Drawn from Aeschylus' *The Oresteia*—the tale of King Agamemnon, Clytemnestra, and their children Orestes and Electra—here the monarch is a Civil War general; his second wife is Christine; their children, Orin and Lavinia. As a trilogy, the parallels to Aeschylus were obvious and brilliant, especially as the 13 total acts reflected psychology, especially Freudian theory. Nazimova rose to greatness as Christine; Alice Brady (1892-1939, pictured) was a cauterizing study in solemnity and pathos as Lavinia.

Whereas today's fiscally straitened theater helps to explain the startling rise in the number of solo artists and small-cast plays on Broadway and elsewhere, the extraordinary talent and oeuvre of Ruth Draper (1884-1956) can only be attributed to her sheer desire to entertain, enlighten, and innovate. For nearly four decades, Draper's sharply drawn, self-written, often satiric monologues depicted society and working-class women with insight and not a little laughter, each encased in Draper's ability to transform herself physically, vocally, and emotionally into whatever character she played. Draper appeared on Broadway in 1929, 1932, 1934, 1940, 1947, 1954, and 1956; she also traveled the world extensively, including tirelessly entertaining the troops during World War II. And when the advent of TV threatened her audience base, she was discovered by a postwar generation deeply fascinated by her chameleonic prowess.

Webb Parmalee Hollenbeck—stage name Clifton Webb (1889-1966)—cut a debonair, sartorially impeccable figure during his stage and screen career. Pushed by an aggressive and domineering stage mother, Webb played vaudeville and sang at Carnegie Hall before debuting on Broadway in the operetta *The Purple Road* (1913). He'd appear in many other musicals and comedies—from *See America First* (1916), with its early Cole Porter score, to the Schwartz-Dietz revue *Flying Colors* (1932)—before being cast in *As Thousands Cheer* (1933), which sported a witty Irving Berlin score and a matchlessly focused and trenchant script by Moss Hart. Webb's uncanny gift for impersonation was soon in full flower, including playing John D. Rockefeller, Sr. (1838-1937, pictured) in a skit called "World's Wealthiest Man Celebrates 94th Birthday" and, later on, Mahatma Gandhi (1869-1948). Noël Coward wrote the roles of Charles in *Blithe Spirit* (1941) and Garry Essendine in *Present Laughter* (1946) for Webb, who received Oscar nominations for Best Supporting Actor for *Laura* (1944), *The Razor's Edge* (1946), and *Sitting Pretty* (1948).

An elegant Alfred Lunt, Lynn Fontanne, and Noël Coward in Coward's *Design for Living* (1933), written for the Lunts—with a role, naturally, for himself. Coward constructed a dilemma set in Paris about a playwright and an artist who both fall in love with a glamorous American woman. Unable to choose between them, the woman agrees to live with both men, and no small amount of neuroses and laughter results. Revived less often than many of Coward's plays (*Private Lives,* by comparison, has had seven Broadway productions, *Present Laughter* four, as opposed to *Design for Living*'s three), it remains a circus of bon mots and supreme sophistication.

The Group Theatre triumphantly scored its second Pulitzer Prize–winning production in three years with *Men in White* (1933) by Sidney Kingsley (1906-95), which proved to be that great rarity—a hit with both critics and theatergoers. In his history of the Actors Studio, Foster Hirsch (194?-) wrote that the drama "about a brilliant young surgeon who, tempted by Mammon, ultimately chooses service to humanity over self-advancement, is a fake, a manufactured, old-fashioned melodrama." But, Hirsch added, the Group Theatre production was "meticulously and lovingly directed and acted, with an earnest realism that had the force of something new"—and it established, one should add, Lee Strasberg as a director of great clarity and skill. Pictured are Alexander Kirkland (1901 or 1908-) as the devil-tempted surgeon and J. Edward Bromberg (1903-51) as the man under whom he may study.

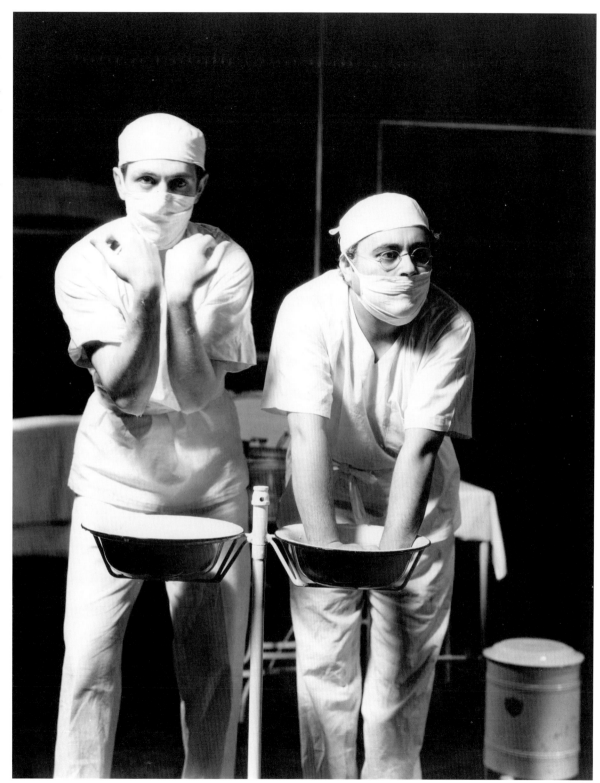

The dainty sign atop the building has been replaced by a gaudy neon tower, and the store to the left and tenement to the right are long gone, but the Ethel Barrymore Theatre remains one of Broadway's most esteemed houses. It's also the only standing theater built by the Shuberts for an actor—which Ethel Barrymore opened by starring in the unremarkable *Kingdom of God* (1928). Signal premieres—out of 170-odd productions—include *Gay Divorce* (1932), *Design for Living* (1933), *The Women* (1936), *Knickerbocker Holiday* (1938), *Pal Joey* (1940), *A Streetcar Named Desire* (1947), *Tea and Sympathy* (1953), *A Raisin in the Sun* (1959), *Black Comedy/White Lies* (1967), *Travesties* (1975), *I Love My Wife* (1977), *Romantic Comedy* (1979), *Foxfire* (1982), *Joe Turner's Come and Gone* (1988), and *The Tale of the Allergist's Wife* (2000). Architecturally, it was another terrific Herbert J. Krapp design, from the facade's terra cotta grillwork to the enormous interior dome, complete with glittering chandelier. This photo was taken in the fall of 1933, during the short run of *Ten Minute Alibi* by Anthony Armstrong (1897-1972).

Of the thousands of plays that have opened on Broadway, only *Life with Father* (1939) has ever outdistanced the 3,182-performance, 90-month run of *Tobacco Road* (1933), the adaptation by Jack Kirkland (1901-69) of the novel by Erskine Caldwell (1903-87). Set in the back country of Georgia, the story focuses on the Lester family, a ragtag collection of squalor-ridden, backward-thinking tenant farmers whose livelihood has not only been permanently degraded by industrialization, but whose sense of values has been forever torn asunder, such as when shiftless patriarch Jeeter Lester, played by the indelible Henry Hull (1890-1977), sells his oldest daughter for a pittance. Audiences, unaccustomed to such familial filth and grit, were mesmerized. Still, *Tobacco Road* has not been revived on the Great White Way in more than 50 years.

Tobacco Road (1933) opened at the John Golden Theatre, then operating under its original name, Theatre Masque. Irwin S. Chanin (1891-1988), an architect and real estate magnate who'd earlier built the 46th Street Theatre (now the Richard Rodgers), hired Herbert J. Krapp to design it—as part of a three-venue complex including the Royale (now the Jacobs) and the Majestic theaters—and the Lincoln Hotel, now the Milford Plaza. All the venues were swathed in a style Krapp called "modern Spanish"; beyond terra cotta bases, Krapp crowned the Golden with an Iberian-tinged version of a Greek skene, or scene house, and studded the interior with other Spanish touches, such as rough plaster walls, spiraling columns, and plenty of wrought iron. In 1930, ownership of all three venues went to the Shuberts; in 1937, the Shuberts handed over management of the house to producer Golden, who'd amassed a fortune by producing *Lightnin'* back in 1918, reasserting management in the 1940s. Since its opening in 1928, the 805-seat Golden has housed more than 175 productions; significant premieres include *Angel Street* (1941), *Soldier's Wife* (1944), *Comedy in Music* (1953), *An Evening with Mike Nichols and Elaine May* (1960), *Beyond the Fringe* (1962), *Sticks and Bones* (1972), *The Gin Game* (1977), *Crimes of the Heart* (1981), *'night, Mother* (1983), *Glengarry Glen Ross* (1984), *Falsettos* (1992), *Master Class* (1995), *Side Man* (1998), *The Goat, or Who Is Sylvia?* (2002), and *Avenue Q* (2003).

The arrival of *Four Saints in Three Acts* (1934) by Gertrude Stein (1874-1946) and Virgil Thomson (1896-1989) at the now-demolished 44th Street Theatre arguably represented the apex of experimentalism in the commercial American theater. Indeed, *Four Saints* remains the only Stein work ever to run on Broadway; it even received a mercifully brief revival in 1952 when Leontyne Price (1927-) was the star. The incomprehensibleness of *Four Saints,* however, remains the stuff of legend: In his *Best Plays of 1933-34,* critic Burns Mantle (1873-1948) noted how its "perfectly mad text" had been "supplied by Gertrude Stein, who flatters herself that she writes perfectly by ear, even though no one can make sense of what she writes, and to this a really beautiful score was fitted by Virgil Thomson."

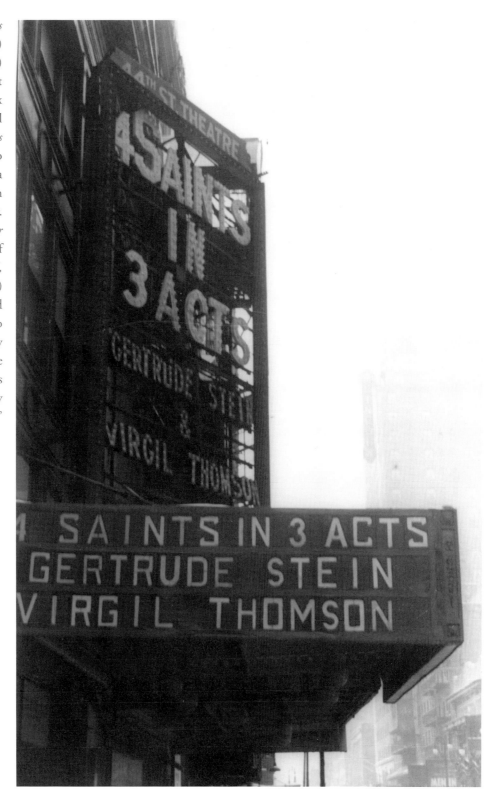

Anything Goes (1934) was inspired by debt evasion and death. The former related to producer Vinton Freedley, who'd cloistered himself on a fishing boat in the Gulf of Panama, a fugitive from his creditors. One day, he imagined a musical set aboard a luxury ship facing possible shipwreck. Convinced such material would turn profits, he returned to New York, satisfied his creditors, and put a passel of theater folk—Cole Porter, Guy Bolton, and P. G. Wodehouse—to writing a score and book. Off the New Jersey coast about this time, the SS *Morro Castle* burned, taking down 125 people. Freedley decided to skip the shipwreck and focus on lighter ideas: nightclub singer Reno Sweeney (Ethel Merman), heartsick young Wall Streeter Billy Crocker (William Gaxton), and Public Enemy No. 13 (Victor Moore, 1878-1962, pictured), who sneaks aboard the SS *American* to evade the FBI. Fast-paced and loopy, *Anything Goes* had one of Porter's wittiest scores, including "I Get a Kick Out of You," "All Through the Night," "You're the Top," "Blow, Gabriel, Blow" and the title song. The original production ran 420 performances and a 1987 revival ran 784. It's unknown just how much Freedley profited, but he likely never again hid on a boat.

Lillian Hellman had dabbled in theater publicity and play reading when producer Herman Shumlin (1898-1979) mounted and directed her play *The Children's Hour* (1934) at Maxine Elliott's Theatre. Hellman based the play on a Scottish court case from 1810—about a pupil who runs away from school and, in a spiteful attempt to thwart being sent back, accuses two of her teachers of being lesbians. The tightly woven play riveted theatergoers, who sustained the play for 691 performances. Although Hellman would go on to write many terrific dramas—*The Little Foxes* (1939), *Watch on the Rhine* (1941), *Toys in the Attic* (1960)—she was equally noted for being the lover of novelist Dashiell Hammett (1894-1961), who may have helped Hellman pen parts of *The Children's Hour*. Hellman's 1952 statement to the House Un-American Activities Committee—"I cannot and will not cut my conscience to fit this year's fashions"—ensured her place in literary and political history. Pictured, left to right, are Robert Keith (1898-1966)—the father of noted actor Brian Keith (1921-)—as Dr. Joseph Cardin; Anne Revere (1903-90), who later won a Tony for her role in *Toys in the Attic,* as Martha Dobie; Florence McGee (1911-?) as Mary Tilford; Katherine Emery (1906-80) as Karen Wright; and Katherine Emmett (1882-1960) as Mrs. Tilford.

Could a play today cause the audience response given to Clifford Odets' *Waiting for Lefty* (1935)? The action occurs at a meeting where New York City taxi drivers are mulling a strike—a common theme during the Great Depression, when labor strife raged. Using flashbacks, Odets explored the bleak lives of these fictional cabbies; when Lefty, whom the hacks admire, is killed by management thugs, the men explode—and with them, wrote Harold Clurman, went the audience. At the play's first performance, a benefit for the Group Theatre, he wrote, "The first scene of *Lefty* had not played two minutes when a shock of delighted recognition struck the audience like a tidal wave. Deep laughter, hot assent, a kind of joyous fervor seemed to sweep the audience toward the stage. The actors no longer performed; they were being carried along as if by an exultancy of communication such as I had never witnessed in the theatre before." Odets and Sanford Meisner (1905-97) co-directed the play, which moved to Broadway for 144 performances. In the cast was Elia Kazan (1909-2003, third from left), who'd appeared in the Group Theatre's *Men in White* (1933) and would act in Odets' *Paradise Lost* (1935) and *Golden Boy* (1937), among other plays, before becoming a landmark director in the 1940s.

Guthrie McClintic's production of Maxwell Anderson's *Winterset* (1935) was a crisp example of 1930s Broadway drama. Written, like most Anderson plays, in blank verse, *Winterset* concerns a young man's efforts to avenge the death of his father, put to death for a crime he didn't commit. The young man, Mio, was played by Burgess Meredith (1908-97, pictured), who had amassed more than a dozen Broadway acting credits since his 1930 debut. In typical Anderson fashion, *Winterset* boasted full-throated drama and suspense—Mio confronts not only the guilt-ridden judge who sentenced his father but the gangster who committed the murder for which his father died. Finally a gang member slays Mio as well. Meredith's career as an actor-director ultimately spanned more than 30 roles and plays; he became famous in the 1960s as the Penguin on TV's *Batman* and famous again as Rocky Balboa's trainer in the *Rocky* films.

As *Waiting for Lefty* (1935) began its run at the Longacre Theatre, the house (named for Times Square's original moniker) had stood on West 48th Street for more than 20 years. Boston Red Sox owner H. H. Frazee (1880-1929)—who famously and regrettably sold Babe Ruth (1895-1948) to the New York Yankees—built the house in 1913, which Henry B. Herts (1871-1933) designed with a French neoclassical facade and a beaux arts interior. It has been a Shubert house since 1919, and has operated as a legitimate theater almost continuously, except for an interregnum as a radio and TV playhouse (1943-53). In all, the Longacre has hosted more than 220 productions; key premieres included *The Butter and Egg Man* (1925), *Morning's at Seven* (1939), *The Lark* (1955), *Rhinoceros* (1961), *Mark Twain Tonight* (1966), *The Ritz* (1975), *The Belle of Amherst* (1976), *The Basic Training of Pavlo Hummel* (1977), *Ain't Misbehavin'* (1978), *Children of a Lesser God* (1980), *The Young Man from Atlanta* (1997), and *Def Poetry Jam* (2002).

169

The Lunts shifted between comedy and drama like a metronome. They appear here in *Idiot's Delight* (1936), which won Robert E. Sherwood the first of four Pulitzer Prizes—adding to it two for the dramas *Abe Lincoln in Illinois* (1938) and *There Shall Be No Night* (1940), and one for history, *Roosevelt and Hopkins* (1948). Produced by the Theatre Guild, *Idiot's Delight* is set in a hotel cocktail lounge in the Italian Alps where a motley crew—a young English couple, an American vaudeville troupe, a French weapons fellow, among others—are ensconced, detainees of the Italian government as war lurks in the air. It provided the perfect setting for Sherwood, a veteran of World War I, to promote antiwar views as the specter of war began hovering over Europe yet again.

The Lunts were everywhere in the 1930s, playing Broadway and touring with the energy of a thousand suns. *Idiot's Delight* (1936) brought them to the Sam S. Shubert Theatre, the flagship house of the Great White Way's biggest landlord; they returned for *Amphitryon 38* (1937) and *The Seagull* (1938), as this image shows. Built in 1913, the house was named for the Shubert brother who'd died in a tragic train accident in 1905; it was designed, with the nearby Booth Theatre, by Henry B. Herts, who gave each venue a dramatic, curved entrance that enabled the adjacent walkway, Shubert Alley, to exude hustle and bustle. Beyond its majestic marquee and billboard, the Shubert's interior boasts classically oriented murals and sumptuous plasterwork. It's also the Shubert house that's least dark; of its 200 productions, major premieres include *Babes in Arms* (1937), *The Philadelphia Story* (1939), *Anne of the Thousand Days* (1948), *Paint Your Wagon* (1951), *Can-Can* (1953), *Bells Are Ringing* (1956), *I Can Get It for You Wholesale* (1962), *Stop the World—I Want to Get Off* (1962), *Promises, Promises* (1968), *A Little Night Music* (1973), *Seascape* (1975), *Crazy for You* (1992), and *Spamalot* (2005). Most important, though, was the 15-year run of *A Chorus Line* (1975).

This image depicts the Lunts in *Amphitryon 38* (1937), a playful comedy adapted by S. N. Behrman (1893-1973) from a play by French writer Jean Giraudoux (1882-1944). The "38" refers to the supposed number of versions of the story that have been created. The piece, echoing the myth of Amphitryon, Alkmena, and Jupiter, finds the latter god in mischievous mode, impersonating Amphitryon and making love to Alkmena, whom Amphitryon is soon to marry. The Theatre Guild, of course, produced, but the Lunts now held artistic control over any project to which they became attached; having built something of a repertory acting company since the 1930s began, they toured yet again in some of the plays in which they had recently starred, including *Idiot's Delight* (1936) and *The Seagull* (1938). The latter featured 19-year-old Uta Hagen as Nina, in her Broadway debut.

Helen Hayes gave the performance of her life in Laurence Housman's *Victoria Regina* (1935), a three-act play that examined the long and eventful life of Queen Victoria from her ascension to the British throne in 1837 and for the following 60 years. Vincent Price (1911-93) played Albert, her consort; their relationship comprised a good deal of the play's evident drama. Hayes played the role more than 600 times over the next three years.

Jumbo (1935) connoted gigantism: critic Percy Hammond (1873-1936) called it a "sane and exciting compound of opera, animal show, folk drama, harlequinade, carnival, circus, extravaganza and spectacle." It was also the last Broadway show at the Hippodrome, a massive, 5,000-seat venue with a 119-foot-wide stage that opened in 1905 and proved reliably profit-averse when not housing spectacles or films. Produced by Billy Rose (1899-1966), directed by John Murray Anderson (1886-1954), and with a Rodgers and Hart score and Hecht and MacArthur book, *Jumbo* squeezed a Broadway-style semi-hit out of the cavernous space. It starred Jimmy Durante (1893-1980) as a thief, and a live elephant. The book worked like this: When Durante tried stealing the elephant, a sheriff caught him red-handed. "Where are you going with that elephant?" the lawman inquired. "What elephant?" Durante replied. Although Depression economics are usually cited for *Jumbo*'s truncated run, the comedy would seem the other culprit.

The rise of new, dynamic British actors naturally led them to cross the pond. After a dispiriting New York debut in the short-lived *The Patriot* (1928), John Gielgud (1904-2000) returned with *Hamlet* (1936), featuring luminous Judith Anderson (1898-1992) as Gertrude and Lillian Gish as Ophelia, which was deemed a success at 132 performances—exceeding John Barrymore's 1922 run significantly. From here on, Gielgud was not only a Broadway regular but a director of high esteem; key projects included *Medea* (1947) starring Anderson; *Much Ado About Nothing* (1959); Peter Shaffer's *Five Finger Exercise* (1959); *Big Fish, Little Fish* (1961) by Hugh Wheeler (1912-87), for which Gielgud won a Tony for direction; *Hamlet* (1964), which earned Hume Cronyn (1911-2003) a Tony and a Tony nomination for Richard Burton (1925-84); *Tiny Alice* (1964) by Edward Albee (1928-); and pairing up with Ralph Richardson (1902-83) for Harold Pinter's *No Man's Land* (1976).

Red Hot and Blue (1936) wasn't a musical theater innovator—or, at 183 performances, much of a hit, even with Ethel Merman, Jimmy Durante, and Bob Hope (1903-2003, in his final Broadway musical) starring. The real story was about ego: While Hope wasn't star enough to demand top billing, Durante and Merman were, and neither would grant it to the other. The show's publicist was thus forced to design posters and ads crossing Merman and Durante's names on the diagonal, Hope's name underneath. The plot was just as wacky: Merman played Nails O'Reilly Duquesne, a manicurist turned rich widow, her sights set on Hope's Bob Hale, her lawyer. Durante, as Policy Pinkie, leader of the polo team at the local prison, is released by the U.S. Congress as Duquesne and Hale aim to create a national lottery, the top prize going to whoever finds a lost woman with a waffle-iron mark on her backside. Bottom line: a top-drawer Cole Porter score, including "Ridin' High," "Down in the Depths (on the Ninetieth Floor)," and "It's De-Lovely."

During the Great Depression, the Federal Theatre Project—sponsored by the Works Progress Administration—was the closest the U.S. has come to a state-subsidized theater. The idea was simple: putting to work tens of thousands of jobless actors, writers, and directors. Hallie Flanagan (1889-1969), a Vassar theater professor, was chosen to lead the FTP in 1935, and she urged artists to work without content restrictions, a move that over time thoroughly rankled diplomats and Washington legislators. Their aggravation was, in some ways, understandable: the Living Newspaper, one of the FTP's most innovative projects, converted articles into performed vignettes with decidedly antigovernment, rabble-rousing slants. On Broadway, meanwhile, the FTP was a blanket presence: the Children's Unit at the Adelphi Theatre (later the George Abbott, later demolished); the Classic Theatre Branch at Maxine Elliott's Theatre; the Theatre of Youth at Harlem's Heckscher Theatre; the Popular Price Theatre at the Manhattan Theatre (now the Ed Sullivan, where *Late Show with David Letterman* is broadcast); the Yiddish Theatre Unit at the Experimental Theatre (formerly the 63rd Street Music Hall). Finally, in 1939, Congress voted to rescind FTP funding, leading to protests like those in this image.

Another part of the Federal Theatre Project was its Negro Theatre Unit. In April 1936, Orson Welles (1915-85) staged a "voodoo" *Macbeth,* set in Haiti, revealing Welles' genius for dramatic derring-do. At 16, he'd debuted at Dublin's Gate Theatre, posing as an actor and Broadway star; at 19, he played Tybalt in a *Romeo and Juliet* produced by and starring Katharine Cornell. At 21, Welles' *Macbeth* awakened Broadway to the brilliant, rising theater artist in their midst. Soon he staged the Marc Blitzstein pro-labor tuner *The Cradle Will Rock* (1938), but a problem loomed: FTP funds were already on the Congressional chopping block and the show's premiere at Maxine Elliott's Theatre had to be scrapped. Undaunted, Welles told ticket-holders the show would go on—20 blocks to the north, where actors performed the piece in the audience. That moment—together with scaring the wits out of radio listeners with his 1938 *War of the Worlds* broadcast and beginning his film career with *Citizen Kane* (1941)—meant Welles was forsaken by Broadway, even when he had forsaken it.

In *On Your Toes* (1936), former vaudevillian Junior asks a society woman to persuade the head of the Russian ballet to stage a jazz-inflected work by a friend, "Slaughter on Tenth Avenue." Junior has a girl, Frankie, but once Russian ballet master Sergei Androvich signs on, Junior is distracted by prima ballerina Vera, even dancing the male lead in "Slaughter." And that's what Vera's dance partner-lover wants for him—why he hires hit men to kill Junior mid-performance, and why Junior dances until the goons are gone. *On Your Toes* boasted huge talents—a Rodgers and Hart score including "It's Got to Be Love," "There's a Small Hotel," and, naturally, "Slaughter on Tenth Avenue," featuring the legendary choreography of George Balanchine (1904-83). The show made a star of Ray Bolger as Junior three years before he played the Scarecrow in *The Wizard of Oz*. Pictured: Luella Gear (1897-1980) as the patroness, Monty Woolley (1888-1963) as Sergei, Bolger, Doris Carson (1912-95) as Frankie. Tamara Geva (1907-97), a premier dancer of her day, played Vera.

Everyone loves backstage stories—how about a backstage photo? At left: director Robert B. Sinclair (1905-70) with the actresses of *The Women* (1936) by Clare Boothe Luce (1903-87). A curare-tipped tale of gossipy Manhattan women who have it all, *The Women* follows these society dames as they gripe and claw in and out of friendships and marriages. Margalo Gillmore (second from left) played Mary, the central character whose husband falls for a working-class hussy. Her closest friends and occasional enemies are Ilka Chase (1905-78, fourth from left) as chatterbox Sylvia; Phyllis Povah (1893-1975, third from left) as ever-pregnant Edith; Adrianne Marden (1909-78, standing) as naive Peggy; and Jane Seymour (1898-1956) as "frozen asset" Nancy. *The Women* ran 657 performances and spawned the iconic 1939 film by George Cukor (1899-1983). Povah and Marjorie Main (1890-1975)—as Lucy, who runs the dude ranch where the women await their Reno divorces—were the only members of the Broadway cast to join the film.

More than 30 years after Rachel Crothers' first Broadway playwriting credit, *Susan and God* (1937) was one of her finest plays. Gertrude Lawrence (center) played the title role, a woman of position who returns from Europe full of feverish spirituality, determined to lead her aristocratic cohorts toward redemption, faith, and religiosity. Yet Susan is mostly show, little tell: husband Barrie (Paul McGrath, 1904-78, right) drinks; daughter Blossom (Nancy Kelly, 1921-95) is a stewpot of resentment and distance toward her mother. In a neat plot twist, Blossom begs Susan not to ship her to another awful summer camp and Susan agrees: the family will spend the summer together, for the first time in years, in their long-shuttered home—provided Barrie skips the booze. What follows isn't between just Susan and Barrie or Susan and God, but Crothers and the audience. A beautiful play. Kelly, incidentally, went on to originate the role of Christine Penmark in Maxwell Anderson's *The Bad Seed* (1954), winning a Tony for Best Actress in a Play.

Direct from timeless Grover's Corners, nothing beats the end of Act II of *Our Town* (1938) by Thornton Wilder, one of the most produced—and metatheatrical—plays by an American playwright. At center is the Stage Manager, played by Frank Craven (1875-1945). Here he's marrying George, played by John Craven (1916-95, and Frank Craven's real-life son), to Emily, played by Martha Scott (1912-2003).

STAGE MANAGER: "Do you, Emily, take this man, George, to be your wedded husband—" Again his further words are covered by those of Mrs. Soames.

MRS. SOAMES: "Don't know when I've seen such a lovely wedding. But I always cry. Don't know why it is, but I always cry. I just like to see young people happy, don't you? Oh, I think it's lovely." The ring. The kiss. The stage is suddenly arrested into silent tableau . . .

Katharine Hepburn (1907-2003) was professionally adrift at the end of the 1930s. Despite winning an Oscar for *Morning Glory* (1933) and acclaim for the films *Alice Adams* (1935), *Stage Door* (1937), *Bringing Up Baby* (1938), and *Holiday* (1938, based on Philip Barry's play), she had torpedoed her progress, alienating the press, Hollywood moguls, and filmgoers. Dubbed "box-office poison," she needed a boost, and *The Philadelphia Story* (1939), which Barry wrote for her, was the ticket. She played Tracy Lord, a socialite set to remarry when her ex-husband turns up amid a plot to expose her father's sordid ways. Screwball comedy elements now ensue in what was surely Hepburn's finest theatrical performance. With the help of billionaire Howard Hughes (1905-76, with whom Hepburn was having an affair), she bought the film rights to Barry's play, made the classic film version, and never looked back. At left is Van Heflin (1910-71) as Macaulay Connor.

If Broadway didn't have Tallulah Bankhead (1902-68), it would have had to invent her. The Alabama-born progeny of the Speaker of the U.S. House of Representatives, Bankhead debuted on Broadway in the instantly forgettable *Squab Farm* (1918). She spent the 1920s in London, a free-spirited, sexually adventurous actress and party-girl—returning in 1933, more famous for her libido than her talent. Of her Cleopatra in Shakespeare's *Antony and Cleopatra* (1937), John Mason Brown (1900-1969) wrote, "Tallulah Bankhead sailed down the Nile in a barge last night and sank." But then, in Lillian Hellman's *The Little Foxes* (1939), Bankhead wowed them all as Regina Giddins, a ruthless Southern woman who'll do absolutely anything for power and money. Later, in Thornton Wilder's *The Skin of Our Teeth* (1943), she outdid herself again. Broadway certainly saw a lot of exhibitionistic, iconoclastic, singular, maddening Tallulah—in every way.

Life with Father (1939) ran on Broadway for seven-and-a-half years, beating the long run of *Tobacco Road* (1933) for a total of 3,224 performances. It remains the longest-running play in Broadway history, and made its authors, Howard Lindsay and Russel Crouse, the great dramatic sages of their age. Based on the stories of Clarence Day, Jr. (1874-1935), the play is set in New York in the late 1800s, focusing on an irascible loving father, his wife, and their sons. Unlike knockabout comedy, *Life with Father*'s tone was quieter, sweeter, ironic, and heartfelt. When the writers couldn't find actors to play the mother and father, Lindsay and his wife Dorothy Stickney (1896-1998) did, playing them for five years. This photo was taken January 19, 1942. Seated is a representative of the U.S. government; the idea was to use this image to sell war bonds (see partly obscured sign at left). Lindsay and Stickney stand beside the bond seller, the cast queued up behind them. Notice the lowered curtain at right.

The Time of Your Life (1939) by William Saroyan (1908-81) was paradoxical—at once rough-hewn and warmhearted. It was another Theatre Guild–produced play to win the Pulitzer Prize, but it was stylistically distinct from all the Guild had stood behind before. Set in a San Francisco saloon, the main character is Joe, a man yearning to better understand his world; the bar teems with such folk. Eddie Dowling (1895-1976), an actor-writer-producer-director of rare gifts, played Joe and co-directed with Saroyan. Julie Haydon (1910-94)—who'd reunite with Dowling for *The Glass Menagerie*—is seated as Kitty, a prostitute. At center: the incomparable Gene Kelly (1912-96), in his third Broadway show in less than two years. Also in the cast: William Bendix (1906-64), famous for TV's *The Life of Riley* (1953-58); and Celeste Holm (1917-), a star of *Oklahoma!* (1943) and a future Oscar winner.

Alexander Woollcott (1887-1943) was a theater critic and radio personality who dominated Broadway from 1914, when he began writing for the *New York Times,* until his death nearly 30 years later. It wasn't about the newspapers he wrote for—the *Herald,* the *Sun;* the "Shouts and Murmurs" column he created in *The New Yorker*—but his rapier wit, consummate urbanity, and outsized persona. George Kaufman and Moss Hart wrote *The Man Who Came to Dinner* (1939)—a comedy about an egocentric cultural avatar who slips on ice in front of the Ohio house he's visiting and proceeds to rule the manse while convalescing— specifically for Woollcott, who initially passed on the role of Sheridan Whiteside. Monty Woolley played it instead for 732 performances. Woollcott, however, did play the venerable, infuriating Sheridan on tour; this image finds him in full-monster mode. Who said critics can't act?

A Pax Americana on Your Houses

(1940–1950)

The Broadway of the 1940s is perhaps the first era represented in this book that a sizable number of readers might vividly remember. Surely there are many who recall the shows of the 1920s and 1930s (their memories solicited), but the 1940s was very much a watershed era in any event. As President Kennedy phrased it in his inaugural address, the world was "tempered by war, disciplined by a hard and bitter peace"—and so, in a sense, was Broadway. The famously panned Laurence Olivier–Vivien Leigh *Romeo and Juliet* might never have occurred had those actors not found safe haven on American shores. The photograph of them enshrines their delicate beauty.

Seriousness was paramount. Despite Celeste Holm's grin in the photo from *Oklahoma!*—and the image of two Billy Bigelows for the price of one from *Carousel*—those shows, the fruits of Richard Rodgers' collaboration with Oscar Hammerstein II, would revolutionize the American musical. Classics, too, were modernizing: check out Paul Robeson and José Ferrer in *Othello* and Judith Anderson's legendary, cauterizing *Medea*. Or escape into the lighter fare: the kooky *Arsenic and Old Lace;* the hare-raising *Harvey.*

With the winning of World War II came a few Broadway landmarks, such as Tennessee Williams' *The Glass Menagerie* and *A Streetcar Named Desire,* and Arthur Miller's *Death of a Salesman.* For *Menagerie,* included is a shot of Laurette Taylor looking pale, almost deathly, giving a performance still worshiped after more than 60 years. Nigh flabbergasting is the image of Marlon Brando, as Stanley Kowalski, kissing Kim Hunter in *Streetcar* while Jessica Tandy, as Blanche DuBois, fretfully glances away. For *Salesman,* take a look at Jo Mielziner's empty, haunted set, a place where Miller's realism and emotional surrealism shocked and intermingled.

Musicals: composer Leonard Bernstein, co-authors Betty Comden and Adolph Green, and choreographer Jerome Robbins and their insouciant *On the Town;* Irving Berlin's penning a score for *Annie Get Your Gun* that gave Ethel Merman (and her clarion voice) yet one more reason to be cheered.

And, as before, some unusual surprises.

The wistful, catchy "Taking a Chance on Love" was just one element recommending *Cabin in the Sky* (1940) to audiences of tasteful musical theater. A variation on the Faust legend from an African-American viewpoint, it had a smart score by composer Vernon Duke and lyricist John La Touche (1914-56). The casting was equally smart, including Dooley Wilson (1886-1953) as the Faust-like Little Joe, Katherine Dunham (1912-2006, pictured in front) as Georgia Brown, and Ethel Waters (1896-1977) as Petunia. All three achieved measures of immortality. Wilson will always be remembered for singing "As Time Goes By" in the film *Casablanca* (1942), though his piano performance was dubbed. Dunham, meanwhile, created one of the first major all-black professional dance troupes, becoming an icon in that field. And Waters was a pioneering Broadway star: She was featured in *As Thousands Cheer* (1933) at a moment when actors of color were relatively segregated from the Broadway firmament. Waters became the second African-American actor to earn an Oscar nomination—for *Pinky* (1949)—and received plaudits acting opposite a young Julie Harris (1925-) in Carson McCullers' *The Member of the Wedding* (1950).

Nearly 40 years after Ethel Barrymore became a star in Clyde Fitch's *Captain Jinks of the Horse Marines,* she was still one of Broadway's greatest attractions. But despite continuing stage and screen success—she won the Best Actress Oscar for *None but the Lonely Heart* (1944)— roles for 60-ish women were, like now, quite prized. So when producer-director Herman Shumlin offered Barrymore the plum role of Miss Moffat in the American premiere of *The Corn Is Green* (1940), a challenging hurricane of a play by actor-writer Emlyn Williams, she leapt at the chance to play the role of an intellectually and emotionally gifted force of nature, a Welsh schoolteacher who chooses to work with poor coal miners, ultimately helping one of them to realize his dream of scholastic greatness. Miss Moffat was indeed the kind of wholly conceived character at which Barrymore excelled, which is why *The Corn Is Green* ran 477 performances and then toured for several years.

Classic revivals on Broadway could fill several books. But *Romeo and Juliet* (1940) was special. "Since Sothern & Marlowe," went an unsigned review in the May 20, 1940, issue of *Time,* "no pair of actors has undertaken Romeo and Juliet with more of an aura about them than Laurence Olivier and Vivien Leigh." Olivier had just dazzled on screen in *Wuthering Heights* (1939) and was remembered on Broadway for *Private Lives* (1931) and the recent *No Time for Comedy* (1939) by S. N. Behrman. Leigh (1913-67) had just won the 1940 Best Actress Oscar for *Gone with the Wind* (1939). Ensconced in the U.S. as World War II in Europe raged, Olivier went all out—directing, co-writing music, overseeing the production scheme. "But last week," *Time* noted, "they saw a Juliet who looked like a poem, but had no sense of poetry, a Romeo who made a handsome lover, but talked as though he was brushing his teeth. . . . They saw Olivier, in the first balcony scene, rush around like a dazed fireman trying to save a trapped maiden from the flames." After 35 performances, it was gone.

Gene Kelly (right) was hardly a second-rate anything, but in *Pal Joey* (1940) he played a second-rate dancer with irresistible charm. Based on the short stories of John O'Hara (1905-70) and featuring yet another indelible Rodgers and Hart score, the story of *Pal Joey* follows the title character to Mike's Club, a smoky Chicago joint, where he abruptly drops his girlfriend Linda after meeting a rich socialite, Vera (Vivienne Segal). Taking to him fully, Vera finances for him a club of his own, called Chez Joey. But after a brush with blackmail, she drops him like a hot potato—she's bored with him anyway. "I Could Write a Book" was one of the great songs of the show, which ran 374 performances; a 1952 revival ran 540. Here's a lyric from another:

I'll sing to him, each spring to him
And worship the trousers that cling to him
Bewitched, bothered and bewildered—am I.

The man at right is Hollywood monster-maker Boris Karloff (1887-1969), debuting on Broadway at 54 in *Arsenic and Old Lace* (1941). In the play by Joseph Kesselring (1902-67), Mortimer Brewster may marry the woman he loves, but how to handle his nutty, murderous family? Elderly aunts Martha Brewster (Jean Adair, left, 1873-1953) and Abby Brewster (Josephine Hull, center, 1886-1957) kill lonely men with arsenic-laced elderberry wine. Mortimer's brother Teddy, digging the Panama Canal in the basement because he thinks he's Theodore Roosevelt—well, that's where the bodies go. And another brother, Jonathan Brewster (Karloff), had plastic surgery done so he looks like—well, Boris Karloff. No wonder the play ran 1,444 performances! Adair and Hull were true stage veterans. Adair's four-decade career was capped in *The Crucible* (1953) by Arthur Miller. Hull's 50-year career included *You Can't Take It with You* (1936) and the stage version of *Harvey* (1941); she won a Best Supporting Actress Oscar for the film version.

Angel Street (1941) was a ripping-good thriller. Written by Patrick Hamilton (1904-62), whose *Rope's End* (1929) sent chills up audiences' spines, this tale was a case of terror piled onto terror. As Mr. Manningham, Vincent Price, adopting an air of ominous creepiness, slowly deceives his wife, played by Judith Evelyn (1913-67), into thinking she's lost her mind. "All Mr. Hamilton and the actors aspire to is a good dose of the heebie-geebies," wrote Brooks Atkinson. "But they have done their jobs like a guild of master craftsmen, and it is impossible not to rejoice in their success." Leo G. Carroll (1892-1972), who'd achieve fame in the 1950s sitcom *Topper* (1953-55), played Rough, the inspector who provides the key to the play's resolution. Pictured is Viola Keats (1911-98), who replaced Evelyn and finished out *Angel Street*'s 1,295-performance run.

Thornton Wilder won his second Pulitzer Prize for *The Skin of Our Teeth* (1942), an audacious allegory revealing man's sad habit of repeating history more frequently than learning from it. With events like ice ages and war as backdrops—as well as biblical references galore—the critics were divided: some believed Wilder stole his conceit from *Finnegans Wake* by James Joyce (1882-1941). Meanwhile, the production also had issues, mostly in terms of Tallulah Bankhead's antics driving her fellow actors, including leads Fredric March and Florence Eldridge (1901-88), to distraction. Even the director, Elia Kazan, wasn't spared the Bankhead blitz. Montgomery Clift (1920-66) and E. G. Marshall (1910-98) were also cast in the play.

That Moss Hart underwent psychotherapy would alarm no one today, but when it inspired *Lady in the Dark* (1942), it was an odd idea for a musical. Hart wrote the book, Ira Gershwin the lyrics, and Kurt Weill—who'd written *Threepenny Opera* (1933) with Bertolt Brecht, *Johnny Johnson* (1936) with Paul Green, and *Knickerbocker Holiday* (1938) with Maxwell Anderson—the music. The plot: magazine editor Liza Elliott can't make her mind up about marrying her publisher or almost anything else. She enters therapy, and much of the show consists of the authors musicalizing her dreams. The brainy, brilliant work benefited from star Gertrude Lawrence, but every time the phenomenally gifted comic actor Danny Kaye (1913-87) sang the Act II song "Tschaikowsky," she felt upstaged. So the authors wrote an immortal song, "The Saga of Jenny," for her. Still, imagine following a song in which 50 Russian composers' names are recited like a rap! Paired up, the two songs brought down the house, helping the musical rack up 467 performances.

For its day, *The Voice of the Turtle* (1943) had an unusually racy theme, helping the play achieve a four-year run. Sally, played by Margaret Sullavan (1911-60), is a single gal conscious of her libido. It's not that she's unconflicted about sex—compared with her friend Olive, played by Audrey Christie (1911-89), who has no compunction about sex at all—but she's certainly attuned to her needs. An actress, Sally moves to New York from Joplin, Missouri, to find her producer boyfriend preferring emotionally diffident sex to falling in love. Olive asks Bill, a G.I. played by Elliott Nugent (1899-1980), to pick her up at Sally's place for a date—and then finds better pickings elsewhere; Sally must salvage the scene. What's next can be imagined, but the virtue of the script, by John Van Druten, is the story isn't played for melodrama or romantic comedy but realism. Left to right: producer Alfred de Liagre, Jr. (1904-87), Sullavan, Nugent, Van Druten, and Christie.

In musical theater annals, there will probably never be an earthquake like the one that occurred after the opening of *Oklahoma!* (1943). Based on the play *Green Grow the Lilacs* (1931) by Lynn Riggs (1899-1954), the show marked the first of the landmark collaborations between Richard Rodgers (leaving his dysfunctional partnership with Lorenz Hart) and Oscar Hammerstein II, who'd often spent the time since *Show Boat* pursuing unsuccessful material. *Oklahoma!* was directed by Rouben Mamoulian, still lauded for his staging of *Porgy and Bess* (1935), and was choreographed by Agnes de Mille (1905-93), who invented the concept of the dream ballet and later contributed to more than a dozen key works of musical theater. And was casting ever better than Alfred Drake (1914-92) as Curly, Joan Roberts (1918-) as Laurey, Howard Da Silva (1909-86) as Jud Fry, Betty Garde (1905-89) as Aunt Eller, and Celeste Holm (pictured), as Ado Annie? One of *Oklahoma!*'s working titles was *Away We Go!* The authors changed it partly at the urging of Boston theater critic Elliot Norton (1903-2003). Its 2,212-performance run stood as the long-run record until *My Fair Lady* (1956) wrested that title some 15 years later.

Paul Robeson (1898-1976) was a pioneering black actor when racism was the norm of social politics. A Rutgers and Columbia Law School graduate, he turned to the theater and originated the role of a lawyer marrying interracially in Eugene O'Neill's *All God's Chillun Got Wings* (1924), and then appeared in a revival of O'Neill's *The Emperor Jones* (1925), slowly building a list of credits spanning Broadway and London. Unable to play Joe in the original *Show Boat* (1927), he did so in the 1932 Broadway revival; his "Ol' Man River," welling up from his remarkable bass, was an iconic fusion of man and music. Robeson's staunch support for civil rights, and more, for the Soviet Union, which welcomed him in the 1930s, earned him stateside enmity. His 296-performance revival of *Othello* (1943) went unfilmed, not only because Hollywood would not show black men kissing white women (as would have been the case between Robeson and Uta Hagen as Desdemona), but because Robeson's politics alienated Hollywood, which ultimately got him blacklisted. Robeson is shown here opposite the great José Ferrer (1912-92) as Iago.

The pride of Weatherford, Texas, Mary Martin (1913-90) was married with a son—actor Larry Hagman (1931-)—at 17, but felt dissatisfied with married life and motherhood. Motivated by wanderlust, she embarked on a show business career that took her to Hollywood and then to New York, where she was cast in the Cole Porter musical *Leave It to Me!* (1938); her big song, "My Heart Belongs to Daddy," caught the attention of critics and theatergoers alike. Five years later, Martin had her first starring Broadway role in *One Touch of Venus* (1943). Kurt Weill wrote the music, S. J. Perelman (1904-79) and Ogden Nash (1902-71) wrote the book, and Nash wrote the lyrics. Shapely, statuesque Martin played—naturally—a Venus statue that comes to life when a ring is placed on her finger. One of Broadway's best-loved stars, Martin won three Tonys—for *South Pacific* (1949), playing Nellie Forbush; *Peter Pan* (1954), in the title role; and *The Sound of Music* (1959), in the role of Maria.

The real shock of *Harvey* (1944), a 1,775-performance hit by Mary Chase (1907-81), isn't so much that it's about a mild-mannered man named Elwood P. Dowd who believes he pals around with a six-foot-three-inch rabbit. Rather, it's that the play—delightful, charming, and eternally in hearts thanks to the 1950 film starring James Stewart—won the 1945 Pulitzer Prize instead of *The Glass Menagerie* (1945), which marked the arrival of Tennessee Williams onto the world dramatic stage. Frank Fay (1897-1961) played Elwood in *Harvey*, and Josephine Hull his woebegone, very understanding sister.

As the end of World War II neared, the exuberant *On the Town* (1944) was just what Broadway needed. An extension of the ballet *Fancy Free* (1944), it followed three soldiers on a 24-hour Manhattan shore leave—played, left to right, by John Battles (1921-), Adolph Green (1914-2002), and Cris Alexander (1920-). There they meet three gorgeous Gotham gals—played, left to right, by Sono Osato (1919-), Betty Comden (1917-2006), and Nancy Walker (1922-92). Comden and Green, who wrote the show's book and lyrics, went on to become Broadway institutions, writing book or lyrics for *Wonderful Town* (1953), *Peter Pan* (1954), *Bells Are Ringing* (1956), *Do Re Mi* (1960), *Hallelujah, Baby!* (1967), *Applause* (1970), *On the Twentieth Century* (1978), *A Doll's Life* (1982), and *The Will Rogers Follies* (1991), among other shows, as well as the screenplay for Hollywood's *Singin' in the Rain* (1952) and other movie musicals, earning two Oscar nominations and winning a raft of Tonys. Music for *On the Town* was by the colossally gifted Leonard Bernstein (1918-90), the first of his five theater scores; choreography was by the matchless Jerome Robbins (1918-98); direction was by George Abbott. While Battles, Osato, and Alexander had varying careers, Walker became a popular character actress, earning two Tony nominations. Besides fame for hawking paper towels on TV, she was nominated for eight Emmys.

During the two-year run of *Carousel* (1945), star John Raitt (1917-2005, right) was understudied and briefly replaced by Howard Keel (1919-2004). Both became musical legends of stage and screen; this rare image shows them in their *Carousel* costumes. Based on Ferenc Molnár's *Liliom* (1921), *Carousel* concerns a cocky carnival barker, Billy Bigelow, and the local factory girl he loves, abuses, and impregnates; when he dies in a failed robbery, Billy is given one last chance to do good on earth. Cast right after auditioning for Oscar Hammerstein II, Keel also understudied Alfred Drake (1914-92) as Curly in *Oklahoma!*, and once managed to perform both roles the same day. Keel later acted in a 1957 revival of *Carousel,* among other shows. Raitt, one of the first recipients of Broadway's Theatre World Award, later created the role of Sid Sorokin in the musical *The Pajama Game* (1955). On the horse is Florence Vandamm (1882-1966), Broadway's great theatrical photographer, with more than 2,000 shows captured by her shutter. The woman in the dark suit remains unidentified. *Carousel's* beautiful score features such songs as "If I Loved You," "June Is Bustin' Out All Over," "Soliloquy," "What's the Use of Wond'rin'?" and "You'll Never Walk Alone."

By 1945, Laurette Taylor was considered a drunken, washed-up has-been, a throwback to an earlier era of stilted acting. Yet few twentieth-century performances are still discussed with the reverence given her Amanda Wingfield in *The Glass Menagerie* (1945). Largely retired since the death of her husband J. Hartley Manners, Taylor could not resist the depth-charged role of the delusional matriarch of a sad, dysfunctional clan (based on playwright Tennessee Williams' own family). Even today, historians struggle to convey the quality of the encomiums she received with fellow actors Julie Haydon (as Laura), Eddie Dowling (as Tom, also the play's co-producer and co-director), and Anthony Ross (1909-55, as the Gentleman Caller). Three years after Taylor's death, Williams wrote: "There was a radiance about her art which I can compare only to the greatest lines of poetry, and which gave me the same shock of revelation as if the air about us had been momentarily broken through by light from some clear space beyond us."

If the dumb blonde is an unfortunate American archetype, few actors embodied it better than Judy Holliday (1921-65). Born Judith Tuvim, she was an assistant switchboard operator for Orson Welles' Mercury Theatre. Soon she networked her way into the *Revuers,* a cabaret act that included Betty Comden and Adolph Green, who wrote the musical *Bells Are Ringing* (1956) for her. Following her Broadway debut in *Kiss Them for Me* (1945), Holliday was cast by playwright-director Garson Kanin in *Born Yesterday* (1946), a comedy he'd first written for stage and screen star Jean Arthur (1900-1991) but who dropped out, citing nervous exhaustion. What a lucky break: the role of the bubbleheaded Billie Dawn (on stairs), the dim mistress of a businessman determined to buy influence in Washington, D.C., somehow suited Holliday perfectly, even though her I.Q. had been scored at genius level; Holliday was largely credited with the play's 1,642-performance run. The cast also included Paul Douglas (1907-59, being shaved) and Gary Merrill (1915-90, far right), as the journalist hired to educate Billie. Holliday won an Oscar when she repeated her role on screen, and won a Tony for *Bells Are Ringing.*

The Iceman Cometh (1946) was the first new Broadway play by Eugene O'Neill—who had won the Nobel Prize for Literature in 1936—in 12 years. Recalling O'Neill's alcoholic youth, it's set in 1912 in a downtown New York bar, "a sanctuary for a weird collection of soaks, has-beens, tarts and half-dead bums—a profane and pipe-dreaming lot given to sustained drunkenness and to frequent self-pity," wrote Ward Morehouse. Inside, Harry Hope—played by Dudley Digges, third from right, in his last Broadway role—heads up the motley crew. Hickey—played by James Barton (1890-1962), fifth from left—once a drunk, has returned; he is "selling a line of salvation," as Morehouse put it. Slowly, he persuades each man to give up drinking and dreaming, to again make of themselves men, not mice. Briefly it seems he'll succeed, but after Hickey reveals he's killed his wife, they all revert to their former state, changed and yet the same. Robert Edmond Jones designed the set for the production, which Eddie Dowling directed and the Theatre Guild produced.

"Doin' What Comes Natur'lly," "You Can't Get a Man with a Gun," "Show Business," "They Say It's Wonderful," "Lost in His Arms," "Sun in the Morning," "Anything You Can Do"—Irving Berlin's score for *Annie Get Your Gun* (1946) had more hits per page of dialogue than most Broadway shows dare to pray for. And at 1,147 performances, the tale of sharpshooters Annie Oakley (1860-1926) and Frank Butler (1850-1926) was by far the biggest success of Ethel Merman's career. It was the only Rodgers and Hammerstein–produced musical that the team didn't also write: Herbert and Dorothy Fields penned the book, Joshua Logan (1908-88) directed, and Helen Tamiris (1903-66) choreographed. In 1966—age 58—Merman re-created her role in the Broadway revival. Pictured at front, left to right: Lea Penman (1895-1962) as Dolly Tate, Ray Middleton (1907-84) as Frank Butler, Merman, William O'Neal (1898-1961) as Buffalo Bill Cody, and Sandra Deel (?-?) as Winnie Tate.

Writer and lyricist E. Y. "Yip" Harburg was piqued by the idea of gold at Fort Knox, then he recalled the legend of leprechauns and how buried gold might grant three wishes. With Fred Saidy (1907-82), his collaborator on the book, and composer Burton Lane (1912-97), he created *Finian's Rainbow* (1947), about an Irishman and his daughter in America who bury a pot of gold that Og, a leprechaun, wants back.

Given the secondary story about a supremacist Senator, it was a charming, challenging show, but the music gave everything a plucky glow, especially the song "How Are Things in Glocca Morra?"

The original cast featured Albert Sharpe (1885-1970) as Finian, Ella Logan (1913-69) as Sharon, and David Wayne (1914-95) as Og; Wayne won the first Tony for Best Featured Actor in a Musical for his performance. Pictured are Nan Wynn (1915-71), a 1940s starlet, and Joe Yule (1894-1950), a vaudevillian and father of Mickey Rooney (1920-), who replaced Logan and Sharpe during the show's 21-month run.

London-born Jessica Tandy (1909-94) had been acting in America for nearly 20 years when she starred in Tennessee Williams' *A Streetcar Named Desire* (1947). Her delusional, melancholic Blanche DuBois earned her the first of three Tonys, and though Hollywood chose Vivien Leigh to play Blanche on film, Tandy, who often teamed up with her husband, actor-director Hume Cronyn, enjoyed an uncommonly rich, varied Broadway career, including *The Fourposter* (1951), *Five Finger Exercise* (1959), *A Delicate Balance* (1966), *All Over* (1971), *The Gin Game* (1977), *Foxfire* (1983), the role of Amanda Wingfield in an all-star revival of *The Glass Menagerie* (1984), and *The Petition* (1986). In this image, the strapping man at left is Marlon Brando—his stage and screen performance as Stanley Kowalski in *Streetcar* altered American acting forever. Beside him is Kim Hunter (1922-2002), the original Stella, who won an Oscar for repeating her performance on film. Elia Kazan directed both the stage and screen versions of *Streetcar,* which won the 1948 Pulitzer Prize.

The Greeks don't usually have an easy time of it on profit-crazed Broadway, but occasionally a revival and a star come along to put the pieces all together—as in the case of the adaptation, by Robinson Jeffers (1887-1962), of Euripides' *Medea* (1947), which won Judith Anderson a 1948 Tony. So intense that she roused audiences out of their seats in shock and anger, she made John Gielgud, her director and her Jason, look meek. Here are the first two sentences of Brooks Atkinson's review: "If Medea does not entirely understand every aspect of her whirling character, she would do well to consult Judith Anderson. For Miss Anderson understands the character more thoroughly than Medea, Euripides or the scholars, and it would be useless now for anyone else to attempt the part." The piece was also notable as the first Broadway credit for Tony-winning actress Marian Seldes (1928-), as Medea's attendant.

Tragedy befell Cole Porter in 1937 when a horse he was riding fell backward and crushed his legs twice; the fizzy insouciance of his earlier work never quite returned. When Porter wrote the score of *Kiss Me, Kate* (1948), though, it was zippy and astonishingly sophisticated even for him. The songs—including "Another Op'nin', Another Show," "Why Can't You Behave?," "Wunderbar," "So in Love," "Tom, Dick or Harry," "I Hate Men," "Too Darn Hot," "Where Is the Life That Late I Led?," "Always True to You in My Fashion," and "Brush Up Your Shakespeare"—meshed perfectly with a witty book by Sam (1899-1971) and Bella Spewack (1899-1990) based on Shakespeare's *The Taming of the Shrew*. Starring Alfred Drake, Patricia Morison (1915-), Lisa Kirk (1912-90), and Harold Lang (1920-85), the 1,070-performance hit won five Tonys—including Porter's only win—and led to a blockbuster movie musical in 1953.

It was on this half-realistic set by Jo Mielziner that *Death of a Salesman* (1949) by Arthur Miller unfolded. At this point, Miller had had a hit with *All My Sons* (1947), about an airplane-parts manufacturer whose faulty cylinder heads lead to the deaths of 21 airmen, and no luck with *The Man Who Had All the Luck* (1944), a four-performance flop. Yet the story of Willy Loman, a sixtyish salesman whose grip on reality is fading, whose relationship with his sons and wife is unraveling, whose pride is stunting his ability to right himself, was a great event in American drama. Lee J. Cobb (1911-76) originated the role of Willy; Mildred Dunnock (1901-91) played his wife, Linda; and sons Biff and Happy were played by Arthur Kennedy (1914-90) and Cameron Mitchell (1918-94), respectively. Distinguished by a stream-of-consciousness structure and staging by Elia Kazan, the play won the 1949 Pulitzer Prize, and Tonys for best play, direction, featured actor for Kennedy, and the first of Mielziner's nine Tonys for design.

This shot of Vivian Blaine (1921-95) was taken when starring in London in *Guys and Dolls* (1950), based on the stories and characters of Damon Runyon (1884-1946). Her Broadway debut as Adelaide came after a career at 20th Century Fox, where she appeared in such films as *State Fair* (1945); her voice, walk, and expressions, though, clearly were those of a stage creature. Often called the finest American musical, the book by Abe Burrows (1910-85) and songs by Frank Loesser (1910-69)—such as "Fugue for Tinhorns," "The Oldest Established," "I'll Know," "A Bushel and a Peck," "Luck Be a Lady," "Sue Me," and "Sit Down, You're Rockin' the Boat"—are classics. Loesser would later write a series of definitive musicals, including *The Most Happy Fella* (1956) and *How to Succeed in Business Without Really Trying* (1961). Meanwhile, "Adelaide's Lament," with which Blaine stopped the show nightly, explains how her 14-year engagement to chronic gambler Nathan Detroit—played by Sam Levene (1905-80)—can result so "a person can develop a cold." Directed by George S. Kaufman, choreographed by Michael Kidd (1919-2007), *Guys and Dolls* ran 1,200 performances and won five Tonys—including one for Robert Alda (1914-86) as Sky Masterson and one for Isabel Bigley (1926-2006) as Sarah Brown.

Golden Era, Post-Broadway, and Beyond

(1950–1970)

In compiling the images for this book, the first photograph, of Edwin Booth and his father, often came to mind. What would they have thought of the stage of the 1950s and later? Would they be proud? Would they be aghast? Would being aghast be a compliment?

One of the challenges in fleshing out this book's final chapter is attempting not to publish too many images from the Billy Rose Theatre Division that have appeared in other well-known publications. The goal here was to find unusual ways to think about iconic performers and productions: The photo of 20-something Julie Harris, for example, staring at herself in her dressing-room mirror, during the run of *The Member of the Wedding.* Rarely do we see great actors in such a moment of reflection and repose.

The high-glamour shot of Lilli Palmer in a revival of Shaw's *Caesar and Cleopatra;* the creative team of *Wonderful Town,* as well as star Rosalind Russell, standing around a piano as Leonard Bernstein teaches them the score; Gwen Verdon and Ray Walston camping it up to promote *Damn Yankees;* the spine-tingling original cast, lined up in a row, of *Long Day's Journey into Night*—these are images of Broadway's golden age we don't ordinarily see.

A *West Side Story* image taken from a distance, making us want to run to the lip of the stage and witness those Jerome Robbins dances; a photograph of Robert Goulet being fitted for a *Camelot* costume, his mouth fully open as if projecting a high note; Uta Hagen looking haggish, slouchy, and threatening in Edward Albee's *Who's Afraid of Virginia Woolf?;* and Albee himself, looking dour, surrounded by the cast and creative team of *A Delicate Balance,* bearing down upon the photographer in a tragicomic evocation of the swinging, swaggering, and sexual 1960s—they're all here.

And yet those Booths are haunting still. How fitting, it seemed, to end this tour with the cast of *Hair* on the occasion of the show's second anniversary on Broadway. What a very cheeky sign they're holding, is it not?

Julie Harris (1925-) has won more Tonys for performance—five—than anyone, receiving the prize for *I Am a Camera* (1952), *The Lark* (1956), *Forty Carats* (1969), *The Last of Mrs. Lincoln* (1973), and *The Belle of Amherst* (1977), as well as five additional nominations. Born in Michigan, she spent the last period of her minority at a boarding school in Manhattan, then was in and out of Yale because she was starting to act professionally—just 19 when cast in her first Broadway show, *It's a Gift* (1945). By the time she landed the role of Frankie Addams in Carson McCullers' *The Member of the Wedding* (1950), she was a seasoned pro—this shot shows Harris in her dressing room at the Empire Theatre. Co-starring Ethel Waters and directed by Harold Clurman, the play focuses on Frankie, a 12-year-old girl feeling a bit left out as her older brother prepares to marry. Harris made her screen debut reprising her performance as Frankie and received an Oscar nomination. She has also won two Emmys (out of 11 nominations) and a Grammy.

This striking image from a revival of George Bernard Shaw's *Caesar and Cleopatra* (1949) shows the breathtaking beauty of Lilli Palmer (1914-86), an enormous star in her native Germany and the wife of British stage and screen star Rex Harrison (1908-90), with whom she would soon act in John Van Druten's *Bell, Book and Candle* (1950). Palmer was acclaimed for her performance in the Shaw play, acting opposite Sir Cedric Hardwicke (1893-1964), the legendary British actor who also directed. In a very minor role was an actor in only his second Broadway appearance. He was billed as Anthony Randall, but we remember him today as Tony Randall (1920-2004).

With *All My Sons* and *Death of a Salesman* behind him, the 1950s marked an intensifying of Arthur Miller's determination to write plays of dramatic import and both cultural and political immediacy. With the House Un-American Activities Committee—to which Miller refused to give evidence—at its peak of influence, the sheer allegorical brilliance of *The Crucible* (1953) eventually earned it a permanent place on the reading lists of thousands of American high schools as well as Broadway revivals in 1964, 1972, 1991, and 2002. Other Miller plays, including *A View from the Bridge* (1955), *After the Fall* (1964), *Incident at Vichy* (1964), *The Price* (1968), *The Creation of the World and Other Business* (1972, later revised as a musical called *Up from Paradise*), *The American Clock* (1980), *Broken Glass* (1994), and *The Ride Down Mt. Morgan* (2000), were the products of a conscientious mind consumed by a fascination with the intersection of drama and morality, ethics and the human spirit. Miller's second wife was actress Marilyn Monroe (1926-62) and his third wife was photographer Inge Morath (1923-2002).

Broadway musicals are notoriously strife-ridden affairs, but you'd never know it by the faces of *Wonderful Town* (1953): composer Leonard Bernstein at piano; co-lyricist Betty Comden; star Rosalind Russell (1911-76), returning to Broadway for the first time since 1931; co-lyricist Adolph Green; director George Abbott; and musical director Lehman Engel (1910-82). It is based on the hit play *My Sister Eileen* (1940) by Joseph Fields and Jerome Chodorov (1911-2004)—itself based on fiction by Ruth McKenney (1911-72). Fields and Chodorov also wrote the musical's book. The story concerns sisters Ruth and Eileen who move to Greenwich Village from Ohio and get into scrapes and romances. Russell won a Tony for playing Ruth; Tonys also went to Engel as conductor and musical director; Donald Saddler (1918-) for choreography; Raoul Pène Du Bois (1912-85) for scenic design; and the show won best musical. Edith Adams (1927-), who played Eileen, later won a Tony for *Li'l Abner* (1957). With songs like "Christopher Street," "Ohio," "One Hundred Easy Ways," "A Little Bit in Love," "Conga!," "Swing," and "Wrong Note Rag," the show easily logged 559 performances.

Historian and critic Ethan Mordden notes that Robert Anderson (1918-), whose *Tea and Sympathy* (1953) raised so many Eisenhower-era eyebrows, only implicates the character of Tom Lee, a young man at a New England boys school, of being homosexual—it is the audience who must fill in the blanks. "Anderson never tells what the kid really wants," Mordden writes, "but the homophobic housemaster's compassionate wife . . . thinks she knows. Alone with the boy at the curtain, she starts unbuttoning her blouse to utter one of the most shocking lines of all time, still quoted today: 'Years from now, when you talk of this . . . and you will . . . be kind.'" The role of Tom Lee went to a young actor named John Kerr (1931-), who won a Tony for his performance; and the actress who uttered that alarming and remarkable curtain line was Hollywood legend Deborah Kerr (1921-2007, no relation), in her Broadway debut. Elia Kazan directed the play, which ran 712 performances. There has never been a Broadway revival.

Picnic (1953) by William Inge (1913-73) finds a strapping young buck arriving at a Kansas town full of women starved for male attention. The follow-up to Inge's tremendously successful *Come Back, Little Sheba* (1950), he was awarded the Pulitzer Prize for the play, which included many remarkable performances. Pictured is consummate character actress Eileen Heckart (1919-2001) as Rosemary Sydney, the town's old-maid teacher. Hal, the hunk who hormonally charges the town, was played by Ralph Meeker (1920-88); Madge, the young woman Hal seduces, was played by Janice Rule (1931-2003); Millie, Madge's younger sister and equally smitten with Hal, was played by the great Kim Stanley (1925-2001), often dubbed "the female Brando." *Picnic* marked the Broadway debut of Paul Newman (1925-), who lobbied hard to play Hal. Alas, director Joshua Logan found Newman was physically inadequate for it, casting him as Hal's friend Alan instead. Newman understudied Hal, however, and eventually played the role. It's Newman, not Meeker, who is more often recalled for his work as Hal.

The Pajama Game (1954) marked the first Broadway producing credit of Harold Prince (1928-), who now has more Tonys—21—than anyone. Based on the novel *7-1/2 Cents* by Richard Bissell (1913-77), *The Pajama Game* occurs at the Sleep-Tite Pajama Factory where a strike imperils a budding romance between a female union leader and her management equivalent. Back in 1954, the show was a hard sell: Prince and producing partner Robert E. Griffith (1907-61), stage managers of *Wonderful Town* (1953), begged George Abbott to consider working on the show. As historian Glenn Litton (19??-) writes, "Griffith and Prince had to collect their $250,000 in driblets from 164 backers, chorus boys and girls, seamstresses, family and friends." Still, the 1,063-performance hit benefited from great Jerry Ross (1926-55) and Richard Adler (1921 or 1923-) songs—"Racing with the Clock," "Hey There," "Once a Year Day," "There Once Was a Man," "Steam Heat," and "Hernando's Hideaway"—and performances by John Raitt, Janis Paige (1922-), Carol Haney (1924-64), and Eddie Foy, Jr. (1905-83). It won Tonys for best musical; best choreography for Bob Fosse (1927-87) in his first Broadway assignment; and best featured actress for Haney. It was revived on Broadway to great acclaim in 2006.

A year after *The Pajama Game, Damn Yankees* (1955) reunited songwriters Richard Adler and Jerry Ross with producers Robert Griffith and Harold Prince, and with George Abbott and Bob Fosse once again directing and choreographing. The source material itself was again a novel—*The Year the Yankees Lost the Pennant,* by Douglass Wallop (1920-85)—which took its cue from *Faust:* a middle-aged devotee of the Washington Senators sells his soul to the devil, for a chance to play for his favorite team. The devil, in the form of odd Mr. Applegate, played by Ray Walston (1914-2001), transforms paunchy Joe Boyd into strapping Joe Hardy, played by Stephen Douglass (1921-). Hardy even becomes the Senators' best pitcher and hitter, but there's a catch: He must return to his wife in a year or lose his soul eternally. Just to tempt him, Applegate hauls out sexy Lola—played by an incomparable redhead, Gwen Verdon (1925-2000). *Damn Yankees* not only scored a second hit for the group, running 1,019 performances, but it turned Verdon into Broadway's newest star, winning her the second of four Tonys. The memorable songs of *Damn Yankees:* "Heart," "Shoeless Joe from Hannibal, Mo.," and "Whatever Lola Wants."

This stage kiss between Ben Gazzara (1930-) and Barbara Bel Geddes (1922-2005) climaxed Tennessee Williams' *Cat on a Hot Tin Roof* (1955). Set in a home on the Mississippi Delta, it tells the story of the troubled marriage of Brick and Maggie and of Brick's family—headed by Big Daddy and Big Mama, played by Burl Ives (1909-95) and Mildred Dunnock. As the clan gathers to celebrate what may be Big Daddy's last birthday—he has cancer, but the family shields him from it—the word "mendacity" erupts over and over, especially as Maggie realizes how sexless and unfulfilling her marriage to Brick has become. Williams' lyrical drama, directed by Elia Kazan, earned him his second Pulitzer Prize; the play was revived on Broadway in 1974, 1990, 2003, and 2008. Alas, the original Broadway production won no Tonys and the film version, starring Elizabeth Taylor (1932-) and Paul Newman with Ives reprising his role, won no Oscars.

Director Moss Hart was upset during Act I of the first performance of the New Haven tryout of *My Fair Lady* (1956). Chronicler Keith Garebian (1943-) writes that lyricist and librettist Alan Jay Lerner (1918-86) and composer Frederick Loewe (1904-88) didn't seem worried when Hart "rushed over frantically." He said, "I knew it. It's just a New Haven hit. That's all. Just a New Haven hit." Loewe "smiled in sympathetic amusement" and said, "My darling Mossie. . . . If you don't know this is the biggest hit that has ever come to New York you had better come with me and get a drink." Indeed, the musical based on George Bernard Shaw's *Pygmalion* (1914) was a monster hit—flawless musical theater that ran six years, 2,717 performances, and sent the career of Julie Andrews (1935-) as Eliza Doolittle into high orbit. Starring Rex Harrison as Henry Higgins, Robert Coote (1909-82) as Colonel Pickering, Stanley Holloway (1890-1982) as Alfred Doolittle, and Cathleen Nesbitt (1889-1982) as Mrs. Higgins, the show won six Tonys, including best musical. Pictured: one of the sketches for sets by Oliver Smith (1918-94), this one for Higgins' study, and including part of a revolving set piece at right.

Some call *Long Day's Journey into Night* (1956) the finest American drama ever written. Set in 1912, it is Eugene O'Neill's autobiographical look at his family, called the Tyrones: his father, James Tyrone, Sr., a retired actor who lost his potential by playing the same role for years; his mother, Mary, a morphine addict; his brother, Jamie, an actor and alcoholic; and Edmund, representing O'Neill, returning home after being a sailor, now suffering from tuberculosis. O'Neill's widow, Carlotta, ignored one of her husband's wishes while honoring another. He had stipulated that the play remain unpublished until 25 years after his death, but when she transferred the rights to Yale University, the way was paved for its first production in Stockholm, as O'Neill wanted. On Broadway, it ran 390 performances. Directed by José Quintero (1924-99)—whose whole career pivoted on his extraordinary association with O'Neill—it starred Fredric March as James Tyrone; Florence Eldridge, his wife, as Mary; and two actors relatively new to the theater: Jason Robards, Jr. (1922-2000) as Jamie and Bradford Dillman (1930-) as Edmond. It earned O'Neill his fourth (and posthumous) Pulitzer Prize and Tonys for Best Play and for March. In the image, Eldridge's gaze is evidence of Mary's morphine addiction.

In *Waiting for Godot* (1956), the quintessentially postmodern, nihilistic, existentialist play by Samuel Beckett (1906-89), two men wait for a man named Godot to arrive, who doesn't. This simple idea forms the crux of one of the most complex, interpretable, and ineffable twentieth-century plays, one that baffled critics, audiences, and actors—like the legendary Bert Lahr (1895-1967), who played the role of Estragon after many years as a star of vaudeville and musical comedy. Absurdism and experimentalism are typically hard sells on Broadway, and that was the case: just 59 performances. But the original Broadway production—also featuring E. G. Marshall (1914-98) as Vladimir, Alvin Epstein (1925-) as Lucky, and Kurt Kasznar (1913-79) as Pozzo—was remarkable for its daring, even though some matinee ladies felt its billing as a comedy was something of a misnomer. The year after the play's Broadway premiere, it returned in an all-black production starring Geoffrey Holder (1930-) and Earle Hyman (1926-). Fifty years later—and despite a 1988 Off-Broadway revival with Steve Martin (1945-) and Robin Williams (1951-)—it has yet to be revived on Broadway.

West Side Story (1957) united the talents of four musical-theater geniuses: composer Leonard Bernstein, lyricist (later composer-lyricist) Stephen Sondheim, librettist Arthur Laurents, and director-choreographer Jerome Robbins. Essentially, the piece is Shakespeare's *Romeo and Juliet* applied to New York's gritty streets, specifically to gang warfare between first-generation Puerto Ricans and their American (or Americanized) counterparts. For 1957 audiences, everything about it was revolutionary: jivey dialogue that made brilliant, lyrical, vernacular theater; a score that took Broadway's brassy sound and added symphonic textures and daring rhymes; staging that used a muscular, intense, iconic dance style to augment the plot and push it forward. Considered edgy for the straitlaced Eisenhower era, *West Side Story* ran 732 performances and launched the careers of many stars, including Larry Kert (1930-91), Carol Lawrence (1934-), and Chita Rivera (1933-). But it won only two Tonys—for Oliver Smith's sets and Robbins' choreography—because *The Music Man* (1957) swept the awards that year.

The brass notes in the pit announced *Gypsy* (1959) as a musical of monumental proportions. Based on the memoirs of striptease artist Gypsy Rose Lee (1911-70), the sister of actress June Havoc (1913-), *Gypsy* paired some of the *West Side Story* team—Stephen Sondheim, Arthur Laurents, Jerome Robbins—with quicksilver melodist Jule Styne (1905-90), a veteran of the musicals *High Button Shoes* (1947), *Gentlemen Prefer Blondes* (1949), and *Bells Are Ringing* (1956). Telling the story of Lee's mother, Rose Hovick (1892-1954), with literary liberties, the character offered Ethel Merman her greatest acting role—a monster of a mother, a torrent of maternal instinct set to one of Broadway's most classic scores, including "Everything's Coming Up Roses," "You Gotta Get a Gimmick," and Rose's unforgettable psychological breakdown, "Rose's Turn." *Gypsy*, which also starred Jack Klugman (1922-) as Herbie and Sandra Church (1943-) as Louise, won no Tonys—Rodgers and Hammerstein's *The Sound of Music* (1960) was the big winner that year—but it ran 702 performances and remains a beloved, often worshipped American musical. Indeed, it has been revived four times on Broadway: in 1974 starring Angela Lansbury (1925-), in 1989 starring Tyne Daly (1946-), in 2003 starring Bernadette Peters (1948-), and in 2008 starring Patti LuPone (1949-). Pictured is a rehearsal shot of an energetic Merman between two of Gypsy's "Toreadorables," played by Marilyn D'Honau (193?-) and Imelda De Martin (1936-).

With the civil rights movement in the ascendant, Lorraine Hansberry (1930-65) made history as the first black woman to have a play produced on Broadway. *A Raisin in the Sun* (1959) was a landmark venture in every way: Lloyd Richards (1919-2006), for example, became the first black man to direct a play on Broadway. Even more, it was one of the first opportunities for African Americans to see their lives and struggles onstage. The tale concerns the Younger family, who dream of leaving their crowded apartment for a home of their own. Acting legend Sidney Poitier (1924-, center) played the lead, Walter Lee, a chauffeur; Claudia McNeil (1917-93, left) was his mother, Lena; Diana Sands (1934-73, right) was his sister, Beneatha; and the luminous Ruby Dee (1924-), today a 60-year veteran of stage and film, played Walter's wife. The original production received four Tony nominations; a 2004 revival starring Sean Combs (1969-), Audra McDonald (1970-), Phylicia Rashad (1948-), and Sanaa Lathan (1971-) earned Tonys for McDonald and Rashad.

Will the voice still be there? When you're Robert Goulet (1933-2007) making your Broadway debut in *Camelot* (1960), yes. Goulet had been cast as Lancelot in this fanciful, slightly moody retelling of the Arthurian legend, Lerner and Loewe's extravagant follow-up to their tremendous success with *My Fair Lady* (1956). Richard Burton (1925-84) played King Arthur, Julie Andrews his Queen Guenevere, and Robert Coote—*My Fair Lady*'s Pickering—was King Pellinore. The production, which ran 873 performances and won four Tonys (though not for Andrews, inexplicably passed over once more), also assembled other *My Fair Lady* alumni: director Moss Hart (who suffered a heart attack during tryouts, forcing Lerner to replace him temporarily), choreographer Hanya Holm (1893-1992), and scenic designer Oliver Smith. *Camelot* has a rousing score, including "I Wonder What the King Is Doing Tonight?," "The Lusty Month of May," "How to Handle a Woman," "If Ever I Would Leave You," "I Loved You Once in Silence," and the title song, a symbol of the Kennedy era. The other two men in the photo, listening intently, remain unidentified.

Part of the writing team for TV's classic *Your Show of Shows* (1950-54), Neil Simon had his third Broadway success with *Barefoot in the Park* (1963), which follows newlyweds in their not-so-ideal New York apartment. The play ran 1,530 performances partly on the strength of Simon's writing—his 30-plus plays, including *The Odd Couple* (1965), *Sweet Charity* (1966), *Plaza Suite* (1968), *The Sunshine Boys* (1972), *California Suite* (1976), *Chapter Two* (1977), *Brighton Beach Memoirs* (1983), *Biloxi Blues* (1985), *Broadway Bound* (1986), *Lost in Yonkers* (1991, Pulitzer Prize), *Laughter on the 23rd Floor* (1993), *The Dinner Party* (2000), and *45 Seconds from Broadway* (2001), have had more than 10,000 cumulative performances on Broadway, making Simon one of the most successful playwrights in history. *Barefoot in the Park* starred Robert Redford (1937-) as conservative Paul Bratter; Elizabeth Ashley (1939-) as his free-spirited wife, Corie; Mildred Natwick (1905-94) as Corie's mother; and Kurt Kasznar as the eccentric neighbor Victor Velasco. For this play, Mike Nichols (1931-) won a Tony for directing, the first of seven such honors he has received.

Since acting with the Lunts in *The Seagull* (1938) decades earlier, Uta Hagen had become a great dramatic actress, winning a Tony, for example, for Clifford Odets' *The Country Girl* (1951). Her next great role, as Martha in *Who's Afraid of Virginia Woolf?* (1962) by Edward Albee, caused a sensation. George, a history professor played by Arthur Hill (1922-2006), and Martha, his wife and daughter of a university president, one night invite a new professor, Nick, played by George Grizzard (1928-2007), and his wife, Honey, played by Melinda Dillon (1939-), over for drinks. Nasty party games commence as alcohol evinces the worst in Martha, who is bitter over many things, not least of which is the loss of a child—one that turns out to be nonexistent. Albee, already the celebrated author of the one-acts *Zoo Story* (1958) and *The American Dream* (1960), was set to win the Pulitzer Prize for *Virginia Woolf* when the prize's advisory board overruled the decision, citing the play's salty language and carnal themes. Directed by Alan Schneider (1917-84), the play ran 664 performances and earned Tonys for Schneider, Hagen, and Hill, and for best play.

Based on the comedies of Plautus, *A Funny Thing Happened on the Way to the Forum* (1962) was the first Broadway musical for which Stephen Sondheim wrote music as well as lyrics. Generally acknowledged as the supreme talent of his era, Sondheim worked with book writers Burt Shevelove (1915-82) and Larry Gelbart (1928-) to fashion a farce about a slave, Pseudolus, played by Zero Mostel, who tries to win his freedom by helping his master, Hero, played by Brian Davies (1938-), to romance mindless Philia, played by Preshy Marker (?-?). Amid the abetting of another slave, Hysterium, played by Jack Gilford (1908-90); narcissistic warmonger Miles Gloriosus, played by Ron Holgate (1937-); Hero's father Senex, played by David Burns (1901-71); and a procurer of women, Marcus Lycus, played by film star John Carradine (1906-88), *Forum* benefited from George Abbott's direction and Jerome Robbins' uncredited staging and choreography. From *Forum*'s catchy opener—"Comedy Tonight"—to the songs "Free," "Lovely," "Pretty Little Picture," "Everybody Ought to Have a Maid," and "I'm Calm," Sondheim's incomparable score provided a respite from the whirligig of mistaken identities and sexual bawdiness that made the show a 964-performance hit and the winner of the Tony for best musical. Bizarrely, while *Forum* also won Tonys for Shevelove, Gelbart, Mostel, Burns, Abbott, and Harold Prince as producer, Sondheim's score wasn't even nominated. No matter—he'd become the most Tony-honored composer-lyricist in history, winning for *Company* (1970), *Follies* (1971), *A Little Night Music* (1973), *Sweeney Todd* (1979), *Into the Woods* (1988), and *Passion* (1994).

Before *Little Me* (1962), the only Broadway work of Sid Caesar was in the revue *Make Mine Manhattan* (1948). Based on *Little Me, The Intimate Memoirs of That Great Star of Stage, Screen & Television, Belle Poitrine* (1961) by Patrick Dennis (1921-76), the novelist who'd created the character of Auntie Mame, *Little Me* perfectly showcased the talents of the man who'd become America's most famous comic actor, on TV's *Your Show of Shows* (1950-54). *Little Me* concerns Belle, a fictitious woman who rises from obscurity and penury to fame and fortune. But the real focus is on the men in her life—from Noble Eggleston (right), an overachieving tweedy sort, to Prince Cherney (left), duke of Rosenzweig, to Fred Poitrine, who married Belle and dies thereafter. Caesar's seven characters and more than 30 costumes made *Little Me* a masterpiece of accents, physicalities, and characterizations, aided and abetted by music by Cy Coleman (1929-2004), lyrics by Carolyn Leigh (1926-81), a wickedly funny book by Neil Simon, choreography by Bob Fosse, and direction by Fosse and Cy Feuer (1911-2006), who produced the show with longtime business partner Ernest Martin (1919-95). It was a modest hit—just 257 performances—but one of the great shows of the early 1960s.

Based on the short story "Tevye and His Daughters," by Sholem Aleichem (1859-1916), *Fiddler on the Roof* (1964) was one of the last musicals of Broadway's so-called golden age, the musical at its most beautifully crafted. Fresh from *Forum*, Zero Mostel played Tevye, patriarch of a Jewish clan in a Russian town, Anatevka. It's 1905; he dreams of a better life, of maintaining old traditions as he marries off his daughters and faces a changing world. When the Tsar's Cossacks destroy Anatevka, he's persuaded to move to America, where so many immigrant tales begin and end. *Fiddler* represented Jerome Robbins' finest moment as a director-choreographer; with the exception of *Jerome Robbins' Broadway* (1989), he'd never work on Broadway again. It was also the high-water mark for lyricist Sheldon Harnick (1924-) and composer Jerry Bock (1928-); their shows include *The Body Beautiful* (1958), the Pulitzer Prize–winning *Fiorello!* (1959), *Tenderloin* (1960), *She Loves Me* (1963), *The Apple Tree* (1966), and *The Rothschilds* (1970). In addition to *Fiddler*'s superlative book by Joseph Stein (1912-), it's best known for its songs ("Tradition," "Matchmaker, Matchmaker," "If I Were a Rich Man," "Miracle of Miracles," "Sunrise, Sunset"); for becoming the longest-running show in Broadway history up to that time (on July 21, 1971, its 2,845th performance); for making stars of Beatrice Arthur (1922-) as Yente the matchmaker, and Austin Pendleton (1940-) as Motel the tailor; and for giving Bette Midler (1945-) her Broadway debut.

Until *The Producers* (2001) won 12 Tonys, *Hello, Dolly!* (1964), based on Thornton Wilder's *The Matchmaker* (1955), was the most honored tuner in Broadway history, winning 10. And while it had the shortest reign of any show to hold the title of longest-running in history (just 10 months, losing the distinction to *Fiddler on the Roof*), it remains an American classic. The story of Dolly Levi, a matchmaker eager to set up various couples and perhaps herself, captured the imagination of theatergoers entranced by the rhapsodic, melodic score by Jerry Herman (1932-). Herman, whose previous Broadway outing was *Milk and Honey* (1961), went on to become the most commercially successful composer-lyricist before Andrew Lloyd Webber (1948-) with such shows as *Mame* (1966) and *La Cage aux Folles* (1983). *Hello, Dolly!*'s title role is forever linked with a pop-eyed gamine named Carol Channing (1921-). The original cast also included Eileen Brennan (1935-), Alice Playten (1947-), and Charles Nelson Reilly (1931-2007), who won a Tony for *How to Succeed in Business Without Really Trying* (1961). Equally memorable was the succession of Dollys following Channing's: Ginger Rogers (1911-95), Martha Raye (1916-94), Betty Grable (1916-73), Dorothy Lamour (1914-96), and Phyllis Diller (1917-); Pearl Bailey (1918-90) starred opposite bandleader Cab Calloway (1907-94) when legendary *Dolly* producer David Merrick (1911-2000) mounted an all-black version of the show. The run triumphantly ended with Ethel Merman— for whom Herman wrote the show—in her final performance in a Broadway show.

Combined with his work on *She Loves Me* (1963), Harold Prince entered the top tier of musical-theater directors with *Cabaret* (1966). Based on John Van Druten's *I Am a Camera* (1951), which itself was adapted from the fiction of Christopher Isherwood (1904-86), *Cabaret* is set in libidinous Weimar Germany; the story follows a British singer's fling with an American man, and the romance between a Jew and his landlady. Meanwhile, Nazi stirrings are detectable in the metaphorical presence and musical numbers of an Emcee—played by Joel Grey (1932-) in one of the touchstone performances of all time. *Cabaret* confirmed composer John Kander (1927-) and lyricist Fred Ebb (1933-2004) as first-rank writers—their shows include *Flora, the Red Menace* (1965), for which Liza Minnelli (1947-) won a Tony in her Broadway debut, as well as *Zorba* (1968), *70, Girls, 70* (1971), *Chicago* (1975), *The Act* (1978), *Woman of the Year* (1981), *The Rink* (1984), *Kiss of the Spider Woman* (1993), *Steel Pier* (1997), and *Curtains* (2007). The terrific book by Joe Masteroff (1919-) buttressed such songs as "Wilkommen," "The Money Song," and the title song, instant classics all. Jill Haworth (1945-) played Sally Bowles; Bert Convy (1933-91), Clifford Bradshaw. Pictured: Lotte Lenya (1898-1981), widow of composer Kurt Weill, as Fraulein Schneider, and Jack Gilford as Herr Schultz. *Cabaret* won eight Tonys.

This curious image seems appropriate for playwright Edward Albee (center)—especially with Jessica Tandy to the left, Hume Cronyn just behind her, and various staff and crew of *A Delicate Balance* (1966), one of the most enigmatic plays in Albee's canon. Not only did it earn Albee the first of three Pulitzers—he also won for *Seascape* (1975) and *Three Tall Women* (1994)—but it proved he was as gifted and threatening to the theatrical status quo as everyone thought he was when *Who's Afraid of Virginia Woolf?* first made waves. Agnes and Tobias, a couple played by Tandy and Cronyn, find Harry and Edna, played by Henderson Forsythe (1917-2006) and Carmen Matthews (1914-95), at their door one day asking to stay with them. Yet the reason—some terror—is never explained, casting a pall over things. Meanwhile, there is Claire, Agnes' sister, played by Rosemary Murphy (1927-), an alcoholic; and Julia, Agnes and Tobias' daughter, her latest marriage a mess, played by Marian Seldes. Directed by Alan Schneider, the production ran four months, earning Seldes a Tony. A 1996 Broadway revival ran six months and won three Tonys.

When Edwin Booth stood beside his father for the portrait at the beginning of this book, he could never have imagined anything as wild or as dynamically theatrical as *Hair* (1968). Subtitled "the American tribal love rock musical," *Hair* has no meaningful plot to speak of, beyond the idea of a group of antiwar, astrologically aware hippies communally living in New York. Everything about it signified breaking with the past, challenging every assumption of what theater can and should do, and would do in the future. The music by Galt McDermot (1928-) was a direct assault on conservative Broadway ears; such songs as "Aquarius" and "Good Morning, Starshine"—with lyrics as well as a book of sorts by James Rado (1932-) and Gerome Ragni (1942-91)—offered percussive, kinetic harmonies and messages that grabbed the musical theater by the throat and thrust it into the late twentieth century. After an Off-Broadway run and other developmental efforts, the original Broadway cast of *Hair,* directed by experimental theater artist Tom O'Horgan (1926-), included Diane Keaton (1946-), composer Paul Jabara (1948-), and Melba Moore (1945-); later performers in *Hair*'s four-year, 1,750-performance run were Keith Carradine (1949-), Ted Lange (1948-), Heather MacRae (1946-), Meat Loaf (1951-), and Ben Vereen.

Notes on the Photographs

Except where noted, all images are from the Billy Rose Theatre Division of The New York Public Library for the Performing Arts. Each photograph is listed by page number and identified by title or description, and the NYPL digital identification number. These numbers can be used to order copies from Photographic Services and Permissions at www.nypl.org/permissions.

BIBLIOGRAPHY

Atkinson, Brooks. *Broadway.* New York: Limelight Editions, 1985.

Barrymore, Ethel. *Memories, an Autobiography.* New York: Harper & Brothers, 1955.

Cheney, Sheldon W. *The New Movement in the Theatre.* New York: Benjamin Blom, 1914.

Churchill, Allen. *The Great White Way: A Re-Creation of Broadway's Golden Era of Theatrical Entertainment.* New York: E. P. Dutton & Company, 1962.

Clurman, Harold. *The Fervent Years: The Group Theatre & the 30's.* New York: Harcourt Brace Jovanovich, 1975.

Drew, John. *My Years on the Stage.* New York: E. P. Dutton & Company, 1921.

Dunn, Don. *The Making of No, No, Nanette: The Incredible Story of the Blunders, Intrigues and Miracles That Transformed a Dusty Musical of the 1920's into the Top Broadway Success of the 1970's.* Secaucus, New Jersey: Citadel Press, 1972.

Garebian, Keith. *The Making of My Fair Lady.* Toronto: ECW Press, 1993.

Gillette, William. *The Illusion of the First Time in Acting.* New York: Dramatic Museum of Columbia University, 1915.

Green, Stanley. *Broadway Musicals Show by Show.* Milwaukee: Hal Leonard Publishing Corp., 1990.

Hart, Moss. *Act One.* New York: Random House, 1959.

Henderson, Mary C. *The City and the Theatre: The History of New York Playhouses, A 250-Year Journey from Bowling Green to Times Square.* New York: Back Stage Books, 2004.

Hirsch, Foster. *A Method to Their Madness: The History of the Actors Studio.* New York: W. W. Norton, 1984.

Lahr, Bert. *Notes on a Cowardly Lion.* New York: Alfred A. Knopf, 1969.

Mantle, Burns. *The Best Plays of 1933-34.* New York: Dodd Mead & Co., 1934.

Marx, Samuel. *Broadway Portraits.* New York: Donald Flamm, 1929.

Mordden, Ethan. *All That Glittered: The Golden Age of Broadway, 1919-1959.* New York: St. Martin's Press, 2007.

Morehouse, Ward. *Matinee Tomorrow.* New York: Whittlesey House, 1949.

Moses, Montrose, and John Mason Brown. *The American Theatre as Seen by Its Critics, 1752-1934.* New York: W. W. Norton & Company, 1934.

Ranald, Margaret Loftus. *The Eugene O'Neill Companion.* Westport, Connecticut: Greenwood Press, 1984.

Smith, Cecil, and Glenn Litton. *Musical Comedy in America: From The Black Crook to The King and I.* New York: Theatre Arts Books, 1950, 1981.

Smith, Jane S. *Elsie de Wolfe: A Life in the High Style.* New York: Atheneum, 1982.

Sobel, Bernard, editor. *The Theatre Handbook and Digest of Plays.* New York: Crown Publishers, 1950.

Symons, Arthur. *Eleonora Duse.* New York: Duffield and Company, 1927.

Williams, Tennessee. *Memoirs.* New York: Doubleday & Co., 1972.

Wilmeth, Don B. *The Cambridge Guide to American Theatre.* Cambridge, U.K.: Cambridge University Press, 1996, 2007.

Wilson, Francis. *Francis Wilson's Life of Himself.* Boston: Houghton Mifflin, 1924.

Woll, Allen. *Black Musical Theatre: From Coontown to Dreamgirls.* New York: Da Capo Press, 1989.

Selected Index of People, Plays, and Theaters